"As authors of a textbook chapter on Geriatric Sexuality, we give our highest recommendation to The Medical Professional's Guide to LGBT+ Inclusion: Creating a Workplace Culture that Nurtures a Welcoming, Inclusive, and Affirming Environment for those looking to expand their knowledge in this rapidly expanding field. LGBT+ patients have complex biopsychosocial characteristics requiring knowledge of human sexuality topics such as sexual orientation and gender identity as well as intersectionality (diversity, equity, and inclusion) and culture topics including health risk factors, sexually transmitted infections, preventive care measures, mental health care, and medication management of chronic diseases. This book addresses all of these topics and more with compassion and respect toward current and prospective patients and encourages the physician reader to understand and embrace topics with an open mind to maximize communication and trust."

Paul N. Bryman, DO, FACOI, AGSF, CMD (he/him) & Lenny Powell, DO, MS, FACOFP, CMD (he/him)

"Through the seasons of my television show "I Am Jazz," millions have watched my interactions with numerous medical professionals. They have also witnessed the heartbreak I have experienced when I have been treated with disrespect based on my gender identity. As a transgender person, I not only fully endorse The Medical Professional's Guide to LGBT+ Inclusion: Creating a Workplace Culture that Nurtures a Welcoming, Inclusive, and Affirming Environment, I support everything Dr. Kryss does to further inclusion and affirmation for the LGBT+ community in this book and in all of the books she has written and will write in the future. This world is a better place when medical professionals and allies stand up for the needs of LGBT+ people!"

Jazz Jennings (she/her), star of the award-winning hit TV show "I Am Jazz"

"It is with enthusiasm that I endorse this important and much needed work by Dr. Shane. Professionally, the evidence clearly identifies LGBT+ affirming care as suicide prevention an essential goal on the individual and public health level. As a Psychiatrist, it is imperative we address the history of harm done historically by our profession by adapting to the evidence and practicing affirming care for our patients and in our care milieu/work environments we can continue to move towards a healthier future. This work impacts many of us personally and can help improve safety and harm reduction in the workplace, encourage and sustain diversity in our care settings to ensure providers reflect the patient populations we serve."

Sarah Nayeem, MD (she/they), Dual Board-Certified Child, Adolescent and Adult Psychiatrist, Attending Psychiatrist, Adult Outpatient Services (AOS), Maimonides Medical Center

"As a medical student I was unaware of the various health risks and disparities within health care that LGBT+ people face, as these topics were never discussed as part of our curriculum. It wasn't until 2016, during my last year of medical school, when I found an article in a medical journal by the Cleveland Clinic that I first learned about LGBT+ affirming care. This revelation changed the course of my medical career. Current and future generations must continue to promote equality and spread awareness on such topics through this book and other ongoing training. It is paramount that LGBT+ affirming care is normalized in the broader medical community so that all LGBT+ people receive dignified care."

Marcus Tellez, D.O., M.P.H., (he/they), Family Medical Physician

"In order to ethically support and provide care to members of LGBT+ communities, it is imperative that health-care professionals are trained and committed to providing inclusive and affirming culturally competent care including the use of this book by Dr. Shane. Health equity is foundational to serving our communities and requires health-care professionals to challenge the status quo, seek out appropriate education based in cultural humility and above all else, be committed to truly doing no harm."

Nick Grant, PhD, ABPP (he/him), President, GLMA: Health Professionals Advancing LGBTQ+ Equality

The Medical Professional's Guide to LGBT+ Inclusion

The rates of medical bullying, absences by LGBT+ professionals due to lack of safety in the workplace, and subsequent suicidality for LGBT+ youth and adults are exponentially higher than for non-LGBT+ youth and adults. As a result, many LGBT+ patients and professionals are suffering needlessly, and many business leaders are unsure of what to do. This book solves that problem.

Featuring real-life situations and scenarios, a glossary, and further resources, this book enables professionals in a variety of business roles to integrate foundational concepts into their everyday interactions with potential and current employees to create an overall medical workplace culture that nurtures a welcoming, inclusive, and affirming environment for all. This book can be utilized by independent readers, department teams, and entire medical corporations reading experiences.

Setting out best practices and professional guidance for creating an LGBT+ inclusive medical workplace, this approachable and easy-to-follow book guides medical leaders and anyone working in a medical facility toward appropriate and proven ways to create safer working environments, update workplace policies, enhance hiring and staff retention protocols, and better support LGBT+ employees in the workplace as well as for LGBT+ patient experiences.

The real-life scenarios are a unique feature of this book. While many offer information, this book is practical and requires active engagement with the material for the reader. The scenarios offer the reader the opportunity to try out the foundational knowledge they obtained in earlier chapters by giving real business place experiences that others have been challenged by. After reading the scenario, there are intentional pointed thought questions, which can be used for discussion if the book is read in groups or teams. This encourages teamwork and shared learning. Then, readers will receive guidance from America's leading LGBT+ expert, who uses her 25+ years of experience to guide the reader as if they were receiving individualized guidance right from her to them!

The Medical Professional's Guide to LGBT+ Inclusion

Creating a Workplace Culture that
Nurtures a Welcoming, Inclusive,
and Affirming Environment

Dr. Kryss Shane, LSW, LMSW (she/her)

Routledge
Taylor & Francis Group
A PRODUCTIVITY PRESS BOOK

First published 2023
by Routledge
605 Third Avenue, New York, NY 10158
and by Routledge

4 Park Square, Milton Park, Abingdon, Oxon, OX14 4RN

Routledge is an imprint of the Taylor & Francis Group, an informa business

ISBN: 978-0-367-76513-2 (hbk)
ISBN: 978-0-367-76511-8 (pbk)
ISBN: 978-1-003-16730-3 (ebk)

DOI: 10.4324/9781003167303

Typeset in Adobe Garamond
by KnowledgeWorks Global Ltd.

This book is for every medical professional who comes in early, who leaves late, and whose personal life includes thoughts about their patients because a passion for providing care doesn't end when the shift ends.

It is for every patient, parent, and provider who worries about whether their identity will distract from the health-care process and whether it is safe to live openly.

It is for the activists who risk their safety and their jobs by speaking up in favor of inclusive and supportive policies. This book is for each reader spending their free time to become more inclusive because kindness and compassion surpass gender and sexual identities.

This book is for each LGBT+ patient, for all of their parents, for all of their siblings who have patiently answered providers' questions in hopes that it will result in easier and more inclusive care for future patients.

Perhaps, most of all, this book is for the trailblazers who know they are superheroes and for the trailblazers of future "genderations" who have yet to identify their superhero potential. I see you, you matter, and thank heavens you're here and that you're you!

Contents

SECTION II   SCENARIOS: TEST YOUR KNOWLEDGE

SECTION III   PUT YOUR KNOWLEDGE INTO PRACTICE

Foreword by Dr. Marci Bowers, President of World Professional Association for Transgender Health

Marci Bowers, M.D. of Burlingame, California, is recognized as a pioneer in the field of Gender Affirming Surgery. She is the first surgeon with transgender history and first woman to perform Gender Affirming Genital surgeries worldwide. She is also the first surgeon to have delivered more than 2000 babies and completed more than 2000 gender-affirming vaginoplasties.

Dr. Bowers is a pelvic and gynecologic surgeon with more than 32 years' experience. She is a University of Minnesota Medical School graduate where she was class and student body president. After residency in Obstetrics and Gynecology at the University of Washington, she practiced in Seattle at the Polyclinic and Swedish Medical Center. Dr. Bowers left Seattle in 2003 to apprentice with the legendary Dr. Stanley Biber, considered the "Father of Transgender Surgery." In 2010, Marci relocated to the San Francisco Bay Area community of Burlingame, CA. In 2014, Dr. Bowers was hired to renew transgender surgery at Sheba Hospital in Tel Aviv, Israel. Subsequently, she initiated transsurgical education programs at Mt. Sinai (New York/2016), Denver Health (2018), the University of Toronto Women's College Hospital (2019), Northwell Health (2020), and Children's Hospital Los Angeles (2020). The Mt. Sinai Transgender Surgical Fellowship is the first of its' kind. Dr. Bowers performed World Professional Association for Transgender Health (WPATH)'s first 2 "live surgery" vaginoplasties at Mt. Sinai in 2018 and 2019.

Dr. Bowers is the WPATH President and currently serves on The Trevor Project Board of Directors having served previous terms with GLAAD and the Transgender Law Center. Her gender-diverse work has been highlighted by appearances on Oprah,

CBS Sunday Morning, and Discovery Health. She has also appeared on the TLC reality series, "I am Jazz" of which this book's author is a cast member. She was interviewed in 2021 by Leslie Stahl for the CBS News program 60 Minutes. Dr. Bowers is recognized as one of the 100 most influential LGBT people on the Guardian's World Pride Power List and one of Huffington Post's 50 Transgender Icons and was called the Transgender Surgery Rock Star (Denver Post) and the Beyonce of Bottom Surgery (KPFK-FM North Hollywood).

Having practiced medicine for decades, I am aware that there are those who question whether transgender health care is necessary or if it is an area of medicine worthy of participation. We're at a point now where the LGBT+ community is more visible than ever but with so much education and acceptance still to go. As a woman with lived trans-experience in an ongoing modern family-type marriage/ partner situation in addition to being a medical professional, I do have unique insight into the struggles and challenges that many LGBT+ people face. While some presume that my personal identity is fundamental to my advocacy for transgender rights and visibility, my support is grounded by the oath we take as providers; first do no harm but do provide care to each patient that is individualized and provided with skill and empathy. Just as medical professionals recognize the need to adapt to new methods and evidence-based technical changes, we must also evolve in our understanding and support of patients' identities and changing needs. While gender variance has been evident throughout history, often it was forcibly suppressed by western "morality" and even illegal in many cultures. Fortunately, we now have research that documents clear efficacy of transgender/gender-diverse (TGD) medical/surgical treatment. Research further demonstrates the crucial role that familial acceptance provides. It is also evident that denying access to gender-affirming health care is harmful to TGD persons. People are people—LGBT+ individuals want simply to live their lives and be respected for who they are.

Although there are providers who fear alienation of cisgender (nontransgender) clientele when they opt to provide gender-inclusive care, their fears are rarely realized. Patients consistently afford loyalty to practitioners who provide quality care to their patients regardless of who those other patients might be. Patients seek medical, emotional, and mental health care regardless of who they are or who they love. The single most ominous development in my many years of medicine has been the recent overreach by judicial bodies, politicians, and legislatures—enacting measures to restrict or deny gender-affirming health care to TGD adolescents. This interruption of the usual patient–physician relationship adds further impetuous for providers to speak out and continue to support their gender-diverse clientele—tell the overwhelming success that treatment brings to patients and families.

Although many health-care facilities and doctors' offices strive to be inclusive, doing so is not possible until every member of the team from physician to nurse to the custodial staff has LGBT+ sensitivity. If gender-inclusive language, paperwork, and signage are not a part of your facility, request that it be so. For providers, The Medical Professional's Guide to LGBT+ Inclusion: Creating a Workplace Culture that Nurtures a Welcoming, Inclusive, and Affirming Environment may offer that assistance. Creating a safe and supportive workspace says to our patients they are valid and valued. There is no medical care more critical than that.

Marci Bowers, M.D.

Preface

This book was not created to push a political agenda, to turn current medical facilities or medical corporations on their heads, or to undermine professional experiences currently being provided throughout America. Instead, this book aims to enlighten the reader and encourage them to consider the ways that small additions or changes to existing medical facilities and medical practices may further benefit their employees and patients professionally, socially, and emotionally. In fact, anything you read even from a source such as The New York Times or find on CNN should be checked against the research and work done by organizations such as WPATH and USPATH (World/United States Professional Association for Transgender Health). Too often, even reputable news organizations lack the full understanding of these topics and can publish material that lack the full story, lack nuance, or may be inaccurate due to a struggle to understand the depth of the material. The same is true when considering DSM and other diagnostic tools which are often not created with an awareness for these populations. As such, this book is not meant to be the end-all/be-all of your learning process but a foundational text and ongoing guide by which you can return for support and direction and which you can pair with existing and upcoming training materials to ensure a most inclusive experience for all.

Your personal beliefs about the lesbian, gay, bisexual, and transgender (LGBT+) community are your own. While it is not guaranteed that you won't reconsider them by the time you've completed this book, please know that it is not this book's goal to focus on those beliefs. In your personal lives, it is, of course, your prerogative to make choices that best align with your personal beliefs. However, this book focuses on choices, behaviors, and actions taken within the professional environment while in the role as a leader.

Some question whether the idea of LGBT+ employees or LGBT+ patients is new. It can seem as if people are constantly inventing new words to identify their sexuality and gender, making it easy to wonder if this is just some silly way that some adolescents are attempting to make themselves seem more exciting and unique. It stands to reason then that these attempts should not lead to any alterations within medical facilities. Some believe that even acknowledging any of these terms only feeds a person's desire to create new terms and new words to stand out more and more from their peers. Others question why there seem to be so many transgender people all of a sudden. Many talk about how no one identified as such in past decades or in previous generations. In both situations, the answer is two-fold. There were not many opportunities for people to live as openly as they do now when it is becoming safer in many states and many countries to publicly identify as something other than a society's typical expected identity options.

In addition, technology has also played a part. In past generations, one person may have felt a certain way and thought they were the only one in the whole world with those thoughts and feelings. Now, because of social media, there are additional opportunities for people to publish and self-publish their experiences, and because people are more easily able to connect to those they identify with, that one person no longer feels they are the only one in the world. Instead, they can hop on a computer or use a browser on their smartphone to connect with others in other communities across the globe who are just like them. Often, this experience allows for a significant amount of validation for the individual who previously thought they were all alone and that the lack of peers sharing this experience meant that their feelings must be wrong, and this indicated that something must be wrong with them. This resulted in many around the world feeling lonely, lost, broken, and unworthy. It is easy to see how a person with this belief could experience depression and why so many attempted or died by suicide.

As the saying goes, there's safety in numbers. This is true with sexual and gender minorities as well. Now, support groups and friendship groups exist on social media, which bring people together from all over the world who would never have otherwise met but among whom shared feelings and identities exist. Simultaneously, video-sharing platforms allow individuals to document their life experiences and personal journeys, which can bring comfort in better understanding to viewers, regardless of whether they feel validated within their own communities, medical facilities, and families.

This book is not about whether there are gay people, whether transgender people are a "real thing," or whether there should or should not be dozens of terms people use to self-identify their place in the world. The reality is that there are gay people, there are transgender people, and there are people who self-identify using terms that may be unfamiliar to others ... and these people work in and seek care in medical facilities with medical professionals. This then leads us to consider whether adults should acknowledge these differences, especially if the adult may believe a patient or colleague is using a word or term solely for attention. Some may even question how anyone should be expected or required to acknowledge these proclaimed differences, as they may remember that not long ago mental health diagnostic manuals considered homosexuality and transgender identity to be mental illnesses. However, every major mental health organization has spoken out in support and acceptance of LGBT+ people for decades, using research and science to buttress their position that sexual orientation and gender identity are a healthy part of who a person is, not a mental health issue that requires fixing.

Now that we've established that LGBT+ people exist and that none of the science-based professional medical and mental health organizations identify these identities as mental illnesses, it is incumbent upon medical leaders to recognize how medical staff and medical leaders impact their employees. Whatever your opinions, whatever your beliefs, it is likely universal that everyone who dedicates their career to the lives of employees wants those employees to be safe and successful. This is the basis of this book. By recognizing ways that LGBT+ patients and employees feel unsafe, unwanted, and unworthy of acceptance, medical professionals have the opportunity to work to minimize those experiences, to maximize the situations as learning experiences, and to help society create care environments for patients and for employees who have healthy self-esteem, an awareness and compassion for their peers, and staff with excitement for the future that they only get to see and experience if they are guided safely throughout their careers.

Acknowledgments

Thank you to my tribe, individuals who consistently choose to prioritize our friendship, no matter the miles, no matter the circumstances: (alphabetical by first name) Ashley Spitler, Bryant Horowitz, Dan Coleman, Danny Roberts, Deb Unger, Gail Vaz-Oxlade, Janet Sasso, Jason Topel, Jordan Hedeby, Karen Uslin, Kat Dooley, Kurt Broz, Lee Watkins (and Sunshine too), Lorena Asadi, Melvin Abston, Porsche Joseph, Richard E. Waits, and Toby Rogers.

Thank you to my Phillies squad; Jeanette, Cheryl, Stacy, Debbie and Debbie, Michelle, Lois, and Sandra. Through our medical mysteries and medical miracles, we remain united. How lucky I am that y'all are in my life!

Thank you to the crew of *I Am Jazz* season 8, who were gentle with me as I wrote this while filming, and to my fellow cast members (especially to Jazz and Jeanette), who not only put up with my ridiculousness but also mic'd me to ensure it ended up recorded for the world to see. Thank you for loving me through all of my silliness and in all of my shades of tie-dye.

Thank you to Dr. Marci Bowers and to Danny Roberts who were generous with their time, resources, and experience in contributing the Foreword and Afterword. Thank you to Dan Coleman, Erica Shepardson of ThrivingInTieDye.com, and Kazuko Giegue who showed up to contribute their unique perspectives to this project via the Resource Guide and Cover artwork, respectively.

Thank you to those who have loved me through my own medical journey, when at the mercy (and when conquering) my endometriosis and adenomyosis: Russ Lottig, Christine Lottig, Susan Mankita, Les Oppenheim, and Benjamin A. Oppenheim. Thank you for believing my pain was real, for loving me when my pain made me less than easy to be around, and for nursing me back to health physically and emotionally. Thank you to Nikko and to Saba who snuggled me for decades, becoming my weighted heating pads, my companions, and my emotional supports, each coming into my life at different times, each individual sources of unconditional love when my own body didn't love me.

Thank you to Dr. Ken Sinervo and his team at The Center For Endometriosis Care who provided not only my final surgery but who provided compassionate care void of gaslighting and full of support. This book, all the books, and everything I'll ever do are only possible because your expertise allowed you to know how to heal my body.

Thank you to Jason Uveges and Troy Diana, incredible men who gave me unconditional support, who were gone far too soon, and who left me with a better sense of self and a stronger sense of purpose. It is because of each of you that I know how to laugh at myself and to honor myself, how to care for others without losing my identity, and how to help guide others to become more open in their hearts and minds because of the compassion and respect you each showed me. Thank you to John Lottig, the loss of whom kept me from remaining lost.

This book is for the firsts who kick up dust while creating the paths that so many have the privilege of walking down more easily, including Ruth Bader Ginsburg (with whom I am proud to share a birthday) and Marsha P. Johnson, women who have spent their lives overcoming the odds whilst changing the landscape of America and the experiences of American women through their unending brilliance, tenacity, and grit. This book is also for the medical professionals who choose to honor us all with the gift of their wisdom via their social media accounts, public speaking events, trainings, appearances in front of legislators, and more. Each of them give/gave of themselves in their careers and then add in their personal time (typically unpaid) all so that the world can be better than they found it and so they can leave it better than they entered it. I encourage every reader to seek these accounts online, to follow them, to donate to their organizations, and to consistently recognize the kindness and the heart of these individuals, all of whom are making your world better each and every day.

This book is the culmination of everything I am, everything I've learned, and everything I believe will make this world a better place. Thank you to those who take the time to read it, who make an effort to internalize the information contained within, and who make consistent, persistent efforts to support and affirm LGBT+ people, no matter their own sexual and gender identities.

How Big of a Problem Is This?

Too often, people fear trying to start a conversation or intervene against negativity. This is not because they do not care or because they do not see the value in improving their work and their knowledge; it is because they fear saying or doing the wrong thing. However, doing and saying nothing implies agreement or consent with anti-LGBT+ behaviors and policies.

- There are an estimated 20 million LGBT+ people in the United States. That's 7.1% of the U.S. population … and that's just in the United States and that's just the number of people who are publicly out, so we know the number is much greater worldwide and overall!
- Of those who transition from one gender to another, research shows that more than 99.7% of people have absolutely no "transition regret."[1]
- 50% of LGBT+ teens seriously considered attempting suicide in the past year, 18% actually made a suicide attempt; 82% wanted mental health care in the past year but only 40% had access to it.
- In 2017, the Center for American Progress published a nationally representative survey of LGBT+ people. The survey found that 10% of LGBT+ individuals reported that a health-care professional refused to see them in the prior year. Those individuals attributed the discrimination to their actual or perceived sexual orientation. 30% of transgender people reported that health-care providers would not see them because of their gender identity.
- A recent literature review found that self-identified LGB individuals are more likely than heterosexuals to rate their health as poor, have more chronic conditions, and have higher prevalence and earlier onset of disabilities. Overall, LGB people report more asthma diagnoses, headaches, allergies, osteoarthritis, and gastrointestinal problems than heterosexual individuals.
- It is estimated that there are approximately 2.7 million LGBT adults aged 50 and older in the United States, 1.1 million of whom are 65 and older.

■ The number of LGBT+ people is growing as more people are polled and more feel safe to come out. In other words, these needs are going to increase and we need the harm to decrease!

Now that we see just a snapshot of these numbers, it is clear that speaking up is necessary to protect LGBT+ people in medical settings. As for knowing what to do, this book will guide you through the process so that you will feel confident in ascertaining problematic situations and policies, knowing who to speak with to make corrections, and knowing how to speak up in support of LGBT+ safety, security, and inclusion in your medical setting.

Note

1 Jedrzejewski BY, Marsiglio MC, Guerriero J, Penkin A, Berli JU; OHSU Transgender Health Program "Regret and Request for Reversal" workgroup. "Regret after Gender Affirming Surgery - A Multidisciplinary Approach to a Multifaceted Patient Experience". Plast Reconstr Surg. 2023 Jan 24. doi: 10.1097/PRS.0000000000010243. Epub ahead of print. PMID: 36727823.

About the Author

Dr. Kryss Shane, LSW, LMSW (she/her) has been called a "Leading LGBT+ Expert" by The New York Times, Cosmopolitan Magazine, CNBC, Huffington Post, various Parent and Business magazines and websites, and by a wide variety of professional organizations due to her 23+ years of experience in this field.

Kryss earned her Bachelor's of Science in Human Development and Family Sciences where she focused her studies on the impact of LGBT+ identities in individuals and within family units at The Ohio State University. Her first master's degree is in the field of Social Work at Barry University and her second master's degree in the field of Education, specializing in Curriculum and Instruction at Western Governor's University. In both, she focused on LGBT+ identities. Kryss earned her Ph.D. in Leadership at University of the Cumberlands where her research focused on LGBT+ and/or Black identities. She holds social work licenses in the states of Ohio and New York, as well as numerous certifications in topics including providing online-specific education, mental health care and LGBT+ youth, suicide prevention, and many, many, more.

She has spent decades traveling the United States and abroad working as a consultant, educator, and corporate trainer, as well as appearing at events and conferences as a keynote speaker, an author, and a writer, all of which focus on making schools, businesses, and community leaders more LGBT+ inclusive. She has also frequently worked as a lecturer and professor at Columbia University, Fordham University, University of Massachusetts Global, and National Louis University, along with being a guest lecturer at many other universities and colleges worldwide.

Although some may best recognize her from being a cast member on the hit television show *I Am Jazz*, others know her from being frequently quote in the media worldwide as a subject matter expert or due to her being named one of Pride Life Global magazine's 13 top advocates in the world. Throughout her career, Kryss has aided in the introduction of Gay Straight Alliances in numerous high schools, participated in the National Equality March in Washington, DC, rallied for nondiscrimination laws in numerous states, and has held or actively participated in meetings with numerous legislators to educate and encourage their participation in the Equality Movement. She has worked in concert with numerous equality-based organizations in a variety of roles to support, affirm, and celebrate the LGBT+ community.

She continues to actively advocate for LGBT+ rights on the local, state, federal, and international levels.

Kryss is proud to have been in a Trisha Yearwood music video (thought to be the first time a rainbow pride flag has appeared in a country music video). She is also a lover of all things tie dye, of NYC pizza, and of 90s music.

You can find links to her social media accounts, interviews and awards, and other information about her, including upcoming appearances, speaking engagements, and book signings via her website: ThisIsKryss.com

Introduction

Before we began this book, let's take a minute to get really real. One of the biggest questions I find most people ask themselves before attending a conference, listening to a speech, or spending time reading a book is Who cares? For this reason, this book will focus only on topics when there is a clear answer, not just to Who cares? but also to Why should I care?

This isn't because you are incapable of making these connections yourselves, but because it is recognized that, by the sheer nature of being a leader, each reader is likely to be focused on many aspects of their professional industry and trying to master them all. In many situations, books that are written for people of a profession are written by people who have never worked within that profession. This results in an entire textbook, reference material, or mandated required reading that works well in theory, but which professionals are swift to acknowledge could never work in practice.

This is why this book will be laid out to make it most accessible for you to find the information you need when you need it.

Section I offers foundational knowledge, including terminology and frequently asked questions. This will provide all readers with the opportunity to gain or review information, ensuring that they are up to date in current best practices regarding language and research.

Section II provides scenarios that allow readers to try out what they learned in Section I. Scenarios offer opportunities to think through various real-life medical situations. Each scenario is followed by questions to answer as well as guidance so that the readers' answers can be deconstructed, to highlight best practices and to gain further insight into the best ways to meet the needs of the employee or medical situation within the scenario. This section can be utilized individually, in small groups, or as a collective. This is a great way to test yourself privately, to collaborate within leadership teams, or to bring a leader-training seminar together to turn theory into practice!

Section III turns the hypothetical scenarios into real-life action! This section will guide readers in assessing their own medical settings, provide scripts to reach out to supervisors to request to discuss making changes in areas where improvements have been identified, and to make alterations within one's own control. This provides the opportunity to discover where your medical is successful, gives insights into how to work with your supervisors to make your medical more LGBT+ inclusive, and offers methods to improve your own office, office, or workplace setting.

The goal of this book is not to make a reader become an expert in this field but rather to provide foundational knowledge that encompasses the immediate needs of the LGBT+ people within your medical work, in a way that causes as little disruption to medical practices and medical facilities as possible. Also, ideas within this book are intentionally set to require little to no preparation time, and little to no expense to purchase supplies or materials. While a reader is certainly welcome to expand any of the suggestions provided or to outsource them by spending money or reallocating staff focus, or incorporating additional supplies and materials, it is not required in order for this book to be useful to you.

The hope is that the information you will read will allow you not just to find implementation opportunities within what you are already leading, but also that it will help you to understand that the nuances and ways of being mindful of the LGBT+ community can cause benefits to patients, employees, staff, families, and to the community overall.

THE FOUNDATION

Terminology and Insights

Section Summary

In this section, you will find foundational information related to the lesbian, gay, bisexual, and transgender communities, as well as to other communities that are under the "sexual orientation and gender identity" umbrella. This includes considerations of safety, allyship, terminology, and frequently asked questions.

How to Use This Section

This section can be utilized individually or collectively. If you are reading this on your own, consider your current knowledge base and assumptions before each section, then read on and compare your thoughts with the information provided. This will allow you to spend as much or as little time in this section as necessary based on the insight you already have, correcting your misperceptions and filling in knowledge gaps as you read. If you are reading this in a small group setting, please encourage individuals to take time to think independently, then for the groups to share their thoughts with one another. After, the answers from the book can be provided, allowing all participants to compare their thoughts and the group's discussion with the correct answers. If the group is large, breakout groups can be assigned to go through this process in a more manageable way, thus allowing everyone the opportunity to share their thoughts and assumptions as they work through the information in this section.

Section Take-Away

The purpose of this section is to inform the reader, to correct misunderstandings and outdated knowledge, and to prepare the reader with the foundation necessary to best utilize the entirety of this book.

DOI: 10.4324/9781003167303-1

Chapter 1

Safety

Until June 2020, there were no mandates of federal protection and this lack of requirements has too often resulted in no legal consideration for the lesbian, gay, bisexual, and transgender (LGBT+) community at all. That meant that each state (and sometimes each city within a state) got to decide whether a person can be discriminated against for being LGBT+. What considerations and protections to provide to LGBT+ members of a medical community and/or to patients and their families were also left up to specific cities or individual medical facilities. With the newness of this, it means that there are likely to be many debates, lawsuits, and possibilities of legal loopholes. It also means that many in positions of power may not be aware of the new laws, or they may be ill-equipped to behave appropriately when they no longer have the option to avoid working with LGBT+ people. This can create situations where different medical facilities in the same community may have vastly different rules, policies, and procedures regarding the LGBT+ community. This information is vital to understand so that medical leaders can be mindful of the life experiences of the LGBT+ people with whom they regularly interact.

Simultaneously, medical facilities and sometimes individual departments have been permitted to make their own rules regarding how to (or even whether to) care for LGBT+ patients, ways of acknowledging patients' loved ones, and how to document these aspects of identity in the patients' charts. The result often created medical environments in which the patient felt personally unsafe or where their focus on protecting their loved one from maltreatment took priority over the reason for the medical visit.

In some places, there are legal questions and attempts to pass bills to undermine the success of LGBT+ people. These are seen with anti-transgender bathroom bills being lobbied to become laws, where there are no clear existing laws regarding identity documentation that supports the patient and their guest(s), and in situations where a city or state has a clear legal inability to alter a person's gender marker on their identification paperwork. In other areas, specific

DOI: 10.4324/9781003167303-2

cities, medical corporations, or medical facilities may have created their own policies to ensure safety and inclusion of support in the medical experience. When looking into LGBT+ people's protections or lack thereof specific to your own community, it is essential to consider not just what has happened within your medical facility or medical community, but also what is happening in the surrounding communities.

In some medical facilities, there are signs or stickers identifying a medical or office as a "safe space." This program has been around for quite some time. The thought behind this, and its goal, is to identify which places and people do not allow homophobic, biphobic, or transphobic language or attacks. When coming out and being out were much rarer, it made sense for the goal to be rooted in recognizing where somebody would not have to hear slurs or degrading comments or looks. In more recent times, however, this is not enough. Now, the most inclusive and welcoming identification is that of being a brave space: a brave-space office, or a brave-space company.

This may simply seem to be a change in semantics, but it is not. In a safe space, there is a designation that homophobic, biphobic, and transphobic language and actions are strictly forbidden. In a brave space, it goes beyond this. Experts have realized that, while it is crucial to stop horrible things from being said, it is insufficient to stop there. In a safe space, a homophobic statement is responded to by telling the employee that this is not acceptable and ending that type of talk. In a brave-space setting, the conversation is much different. Instead of shutting the conversation down, those in brave spaces encourage further discussion about what has been said or done. Rather than saying that it is not acceptable to use a word or phrase, it is asked why the person chose to use that word or phrase. The focus is not on shutting down the communication; it is on nurturing the communication so as to better understand the perspective of that person, and to encourage them to think through where their thoughts and ideas originate. Whether these are biased or bigoted, and no matter how overarching these ideas and ideals are, starting the conversation where that person is at allows the speaker an opportunity to recognize the impact of their words, to consider where their assumptions began, and to make sure that what they have said is what they genuinely feel and intend when they are using this type of language.

In a medical setting, this may be somewhat tricky, because it is not always possible for a leader to stop an entire meeting or conference or to interrupt someone speaking with a patient to talk through this process with one employee or provider. It makes sense then that a safe-space protocol is used, as it is much more efficient to tell an employee to be quiet than it would be to sit with them and talk through why they said what they did. (In some cases though, it may be wise to allow a patient to see an immediate refusal to allow one person to speak to them inaccurately as a way to both stop the harm and to indicate that the one inaccurate or rude provider does not represent the full extent of the care experience that the patient should expect to receive from the facility.)

In times when it is inappropriate to address the situation immediately, these types of conversations can occur during a break, in a private space before or after medical hours, or, depending on your role and your industry, you may be in a position to require an employee to have a documented correction plan entered into their employment file that includes assigning them to write a document that clarifies their words or requires them to research their incorrect assumptions about the person or group of people they spoke poorly about. In some offices, it may be best to establish a planned protocol at the beginning of the company's creation or alter current onboarding and continuing education policies to indicate all rules and expectations that employees must follow, including nondiscrimination and hostile work environment topic coverage.

When we look at the idea of safety, we must consider who is being kept safe. Politically, this can be a topic of significant debate. Often, this debate boils down to the difference between those who believes that people should not be forced to hear, see, or experience bigotry, and those who believe that shielding employees from this experience makes them ill-prepared to deal with the real world and the things that people may say in public spaces or during their careers. It can be easy for a conversation about safety to become a conversation and debate over one side or the other. However, this is not necessary, nor is it helpful to patients, patients' loved ones, employees, or medical leaders.

This can lead to discussions about what safety measures are realistic. While some may feel that there should be significant opportunities for LGBT+ employees and/or employees of other minority groups to lead these conversations, this is not often possible. It is necessary as a leader to recognize that those in a position to make decisions about budgets may not be able to allocate programming or funds to one specific minority group within the medical. However, it cannot be that nothing is done because action is said to be "unaffordable." Instead, it is necessary to consider what changes and improvements can be made with little to no cost and with little to no change in the daily interactions of employees and staff. These recommendations are much more likely to be approved by those in positions of power because they cause very little, if any, upset to predetermined budgets or to how medical leaders and employees typically behave. This is not instead of changes and improvements that require cost but as an immediate process while working toward the additional changes requiring a longer time to implement due to budgets, construction, or other logistical realities.

Medical leaders should also refer to existing medical rules and policies. If there is already something in place regarding bullying, verbal assault, or physical assault, creating inclusion for LGBT+ people by making small changes becomes very simple. In some medical facilities, support for LGBT+ people would be listed as a separate item within the medical rules and guidelines. In other medical facilities, they simply add the language "sexual orientation and gender identity or expression" to rules that already list the types of bigotry or harassment that may exist, and which are not permitted. In today's society, most medical facilities already have policies in place regarding sexually explicit words and actions, as well as gender biases, so including "sexual orientation and gender identity or expression" or replacing previous words with these can make this policy much more inclusive, with very little change. This can result in a reasonably quick alteration without significant discussion or concern by medical leadership board or existing staff.

In addition to this set of rules being a requirement of employees to understand and follow, medical facilities typically mandate medical leaders be mindful of the rules and be held accountable for following them. Usually, this is because medical facilities believe that medical leaders are automatic role models and that following these rules is simply modeling appropriate adult behavior and interaction, which betters the medical experience for everyone. It may be necessary to alert all staff in the community when a policy change is made or when additional words are added to existing policies. This allows everyone to recognize the change, and this will also enable medical leaders and staff to be held accountable if they break these rules. These not only protect all LGBT+ employees, but they also protect LGBT+ medical partners, and LGBT+ members of the community who may interact with the medical through volunteer work, attending medical or networking events, and/or those who advertise with the medical in local school academic award programs, athletic sponsorship, or when donating for medical events. This protection keeps everyone physically and psychologically safe from discrimination and bigotry in medical settings and at medical events.

Chapter 2

Hate Crimes

As we move through this book, we must acknowledge the ongoing experience of hate crimes. Some of these occur daily and go too often unreported, such as assaults and murders of Black transgender women. Others become nationwide news such as the targeted mass shootings that occurred at Pulse nightclub and Club Q, where an outsider entered an LGBT+ space with an automatic weapon and murdered many while injuring others. When these events occur, it is critical that we are mindful of their impact not only on those who are physically harmed and the local community but also on everyone who hears this news nationally and worldwide. Each time the news story plays or is discussed, it reminds LGBT+ people that they are not safe, that they cannot come together in groups, and that who they are inherently make them a target. In addition, the public's reactions to these events are also significantly impactful. In some cases, this is encouraging and inspiring when politicians work to immediately speak up in support of the community, when they enact legislation to protect the community, and when donations are made to encourage the rebuilding or furthering of community spaces for inclusion. In other cases, politicians, news reporters, and those in an LGBT+ individual's personal life can intensify the pain by belittling the situation, making disgusting comments about the event, misgendering and making harmful comments about the victim(s), or otherwise making light of a very dark and very heavy situation that deserves significant respect and an immediate response.

The anxiety, depression, sadness, insomnia, changes in eating or weight, and other symptoms you may see in others and/or that you may personally experience in reaction to hate crime are to be expected and should be attended to as compassionately as possible. It is in these times that allyship is also critical as the overall messaging cannot simply be that it is unsafe to be who they are but also that there are those who will and do speak up for them and will stand with them. Sometimes, allies do not know what to do or say in these moments of intense sadness and grief. Next, we will look at what allyship is and talk through how each person can use their inherent skills and their natural personality to do the best they can to support this community, both during times of attack and mourning and every single day.

DOI: 10.4324/9781003167303-3

Chapter 3

Allyship

Why It Matters That You Are an LGBT+ Ally

Several medical professionals may question whether there is a need for reading this book. These are typically either those who have personal feelings and beliefs about the LGBT+ community or those who already identify themselves as LGBT+ supporters. Those who have personal opinions and beliefs must recognize that it is against codes of conduct and professional codes of ethics to do less for one group of employees than another or to allow one's personal beliefs or opinions to negatively influence the experience that patients or employees receive. It is also likely in the contract signed to commit to a leadership role within a company that there is something in the policy that prevents medical professionals from adversely interacting with patients, employees, staff, and community members based on their minority status(es). This means that even if a reader of this book has powerful beliefs against the LGBT+ community or against employees who self-identify as LGBT+, it is not permissible to avoid this topic. Instead, the information within this book can help both those with negative beliefs with opposition and those who already identify as LGBT+ supporters to best understand how to use their platform as medical leaders to provide the best possible environment and experience for all, including the LGBT+ community.

The idea of identifying as an ally of any marginalized group of people is not new. While many may consider themselves to be an "LGBT+ ally," there is a significant difference across the spectrum of ally identities. For others, this book may require more introspection to identify how and why their personal beliefs, opinions, and actions may influence their treatment of LGBT+ employees, medical staff, and medical community leaders. Regardless of what identity a reader of this book wears, being mindful of that identity is not enough. Instead, we must examine what it means to be someone who supports the LGBT+ community, whether this is due to a personal conviction or mandates by the profession, the medical community, and/or policies and laws.

DOI: 10.4324/9781003167303-4

This leads to questioning who qualifies as an ally. What makes a person qualified to identify as someone supportive of this community? This is something that may be debatable. In some cases, a person may identify themselves as an ally by simply not going out of their way to harm an LGBT+ person. Others may think that their ally status applies because they vote in each election in favor of inclusive policies. While neither of these is incorrect, and both benefit the LGBT+ community, this is not enough. Some debate whether the word "ally" is the best descriptor of a person regarding the LGBT+ community and their impact on it. While "ally" is the most commonly used word, some use the word "advocate," which implies much more of an active experience. To be an ally simply means to not go against this group of people. To be an advocate would acknowledge speaking up with or for LGBT+ people in situations where there may not be an LGBT+ person present, or where it may not be safe for an LGBT+ person to be out. Those who do more may be considered an "activist." Typically, this is a person who participates in different layers and levels of supporting the LGBT+ community. This may mean that the person talks with medical boards or local, state, or federal politicians regarding better protections for LGBT+ people. In organizations that actively work to prevent equality for LGBT+ people, allies, advocates, and activists may be referred to as "accomplices." In the same way that a person who commits a crime may have an accomplice who helps them to commit a crime, the word "accomplice" is used to draw negative connotations to anyone who works to support the LGBT+ community.

Who Am I and What Traits Do I Bring to Allyship?

Often, the concept of being an ally is brought about in one of two ways, either as a passive construct "just don't behave in ways that harm a group of people" or in an aggressive construct "scream as loudly as possible when you observe bigotry or mistreatment." Typically, neither option feels like a fit for most people, leaving the majority to either be unclear how they can be an ally or to cause people to not know what to do and thus decide that it is better to do nothing than to do the wrong thing.

As you spend time learning and growing within the pages of this book, it will be important that you consider how you will engage with the material as you envision yourself utilizing what is taught. It is encouraged that you consider who you are and what traits come most naturally to you. Here are some descriptive words that may be how you see yourself and ways in which you may find it most natural for you to channel your new knowledge and your new role as an ally.

First to Speak Up in a Meeting, Happy to Share Your Ideas with Leadership, Excited by the Chance to Present at a Conference

Your allyship may be loud and proud! You may find a desire to attend rallies, participate in protests, or you may seek out opportunities to sit on boards or committees at work or within your community to support inclusion. You might even decide to create programming in your workplace to measure the efficacy of more inclusion, with the plan to present your findings as an industry event where others may adopt your methods.

You may be seen as someone who speaks up and calls out disrespectful conversations and holds your colleagues accountable. LGBT+ people may see you as a safe person in the workplace because you never make them feel alone in moments when another employee is saying or doing something homophobic or transphobic. Your actions help LGBT+ employees feel seen, heard, and valued. It can be what lessens workplace bullying and may even save a life.

The Go-To When Something Needs to Be Done Right, Always Relied upon by Others on the Team, the Boss' Right Hand

You may not be someone who speaks up in any format but your ability to put what you learn into practice is impressive! You'll be the one who uses the information within this book to inform your behaviors and you will naturally seek out ways to alter existing policies and procedures within your workplace.

You may be seen as someone who helps the boss to see where company culture can improve. It may be your voice in the boss' ear that helps them to reassess how the employees treat LGBT+ colleagues, ensuring that sexual and gender minorities do not become left out or ostracized in the workplace. Your actions help LGBT+ employees feel seen, heard, and valued. It can be what lessens workplace bullying and may even save a life.

Not a Fan of Team Meetings But Great One-on-One, More Likely to Write Thoughts Down Than to Voice Them, More of an Observer Than a Talker

When you hear or observe someone behaving badly or making comments out of ignorance, you excel in taking the person aside and helping them to see the errors in their ways without making them feel embarrassed! You might do this by using your words or by quietly giving them a copy of this book. You may be best able to be an ally by writing e-mails to decision-makers and lawmakers within your community and state. While you are not the first to speak up, you are often the wise one that others come to for guidance before making a company-wide change, making your allyship crucial to the collective.

You may be seen as the point person for new inclusion policies. Your ability to oversee groups of people and to observe without reacting may be what helps the entire office or company become more mindful of areas where they need to improve and ways in which LGBT+ people may be better included in the growth and goals of the company. Your actions help LGBT+ employees feel seen, heard, and valued. It can be what lessens workplace bullying and may even save a life.

Some of you may have found that you fit into more than one category, resulting in even more ideas and ways to be a supportive ally. Others of you may have noticed that, regardless of the behaviors that most likely fit your personality type and role, you were told that your actions help LGBT+ employees feel seen, heard, and valued. It can be what lessens workplace bullying and may even save a life. This is because there is no one way to be a great LGBT+ ally. Each of these actions helps. Each time you act helps. An LGBT+ person does not just need or deserve your support in the workplace once or twice, but all the time, until confirmed changes occur within the culture and the acceptable behaviors of everyone. The more you use your inherent gifts and talents to support someone in a way that feels most natural to you, the better the workplace is for everyone of every background and identity. Your contribution to that experience not only aligns with compassion and strong leadership skills in that moment, but it may also reverberate throughout the workplace and may be long held in the heart of the person your words or actions supported.

How to Be an Active Ally

How do you let people know that you are supportive? This is something that is much more introspective. Although we've discussed when this support is mandated by your profession, by your professional association, and by the rules and regulations you agreed to in order to become a leader in your specific medical, how you support and how you let people know that you support is much more personal.

This leads us to consider how much you will stand up in support of the LGBT+ community. Is there something you are willing to say, but if you get a certain amount of pushback, you will sit quietly? This can cause us to ask: What are you willing to risk? Is there a line for you regarding who you are willing to upset, or how much you are willing to speak up and where you could be silenced? This is not rooted in judgment; different people have different priorities.

In some cases, it might be less risky for a person who has additional income to speak more loudly in support of the LGBT+ community because they are not financially risking their ability to pay their bills. In other situations, a person may have to choose whether to risk being suspended or terminated at work to support the LGBT+ community. While this is not intended to create a hierarchy of support among you and your colleagues, this is an internal or even a family conversation you may wish to have in advance so that you can make these decisions during a time at home rather than in the middle of a debate or problem situation.

Another question to consider is whether you would be willing to accept the stigma that comes with an LGBT+ identity. Often, our society believes that people only fight for those who are like them. It can cause people to question the personal identity of allies, advocates, or activists working for any marginalized groups. However, it is often much easier to see a person not identifying with a group they support when this differentiation is visible and prominent. For example, a white person participating in a protest or discussion for Black Lives Matter does not at any time appear to be a person of color. Since identifying as LGBT+ is not always visually apparent, supporting this community may cause some to make assumptions about one's sexual orientation or gender identity. Thus, it is essential to consider how far you may be willing to go to support a community and at what point, if ever, you will feel the need to separate yourself from the community by making it clear to others that you are not a member of that community.

In some cases, this may feel like simply being honest or even showing others that this population deserves support and acceptance from everyone, not just from other LGBT+ people. In different situations, becoming vocal about one's own gender identity or sexual orientation becomes a way to lessen the risk or minimize any backlash of participation of support. Again, there may not be a correct answer, but this is something you may wish to think through or talk through before events occur in which decisions would need to be made on this topic.

Let's look at mistakes that are often made by those who do indeed mean well and are supportive of LGBT+ people. This is not intended to cause you to second guess your support in the future, or to come down hard on yourself if you realize anything that follows may indicate a mistake you have made in the past. This is intended to shine a light on areas that may not have been highlighted and to provide new considerations for supportive behaviors moving forward.

Do you tell your colleagues if somebody identifies as LGBT+? Is this something that you tell because it is exciting gossip? Is this something that you discuss with the intention of preventing somebody from making a homophobic, biphobic, or transphobic comment in front of a person who identifies as LGBT+? While the aim here may be right, it is never appropriate to talk about a person's sexuality or their gender unless they have given you specific permission to do so. Although you may mean well, this can create situations in which safety may become an issue for an LGBT+ person because there are some who do become violent, and because it means that the LGBT+ person does not know exactly who is aware of their identity. In addition, many states of America still allow a person to be fired for identifying as LGBT+. Even in cases where you think you are being helpful and where you absolutely mean well, outing an LGBT+ person at any time can put them at significant risk. Outing them in a workplace or to anyone who also works there can result in them losing their job. While this may not seem like a realistic situation because you know your colleagues, it is not always clear whose personal beliefs may cause them to create problems for an LGBT+ person.

Do you support equality specifically for the accolades and praise? While many people like to complete volunteer work or attend events in support of a minority group, it is essential to consider whether you would continue to support these organizations, people, and events even if you were never thanked, noticed, or praised for your support. Do you speak up when you hear bigotry? With its ongoing and consistent reports of violence against those in the LGBT+ community, the news has made it clear how frequently hate crimes occur. This means that anyone speaking up to support LGBT+ people in a public setting is taking a risk. This may be a minimal risk, or it may be more serious—for example, when involved in witnessing a violent act or some type of harassment against LGBT+ people. Do you have a line at which you stop supporting and stop helping? Acknowledging this in advance can help to prepare you for situations where you may have something occurring in front of you.

Too often, people do not think through what they would do in a situation until they are in that situation. That can lead to feeling uncertain of how to respond or not responding at all. In these situations, someone's safety may be directly threatened.

Knowing in advance how you would respond can help the person being victimized either because you choose to step in or because you are quickly able to find an alternative solution to help that person. Another consideration is whether and how much you would speak up in support of LGBT+ employees and colleagues when it comes to your own family. It is common for people to be willing to step up or speak up when something is occurring in a public space between strangers. This is often because right and wrong can appear obvious. Plus, many people are not very concerned with what a stranger may think if they speak up. However, what about your own loved ones? Do you speak up if your spouse or staff member says something against LGBT+ people in their workplace or medical? Do you speak up at a holiday meal when someone in your extended family says something negative about LGBT+ people? Often, there are no clear-cut answers. However, this may be a conversation to have with those you are closest to in advance, or before a large family gathering. In some cases, it may not make sense to challenge a grandparent in the moment. However, you may make the decision to address it with that person and with others at a different time.

Being mindful of this before the event can help to prevent anyone from believing that your silence in the moment equals an agreement to what was just said. Finally, do you self-identify to make sure that bigoted people know that you are not an LGBT+ person? While it may be intentional to identify otherwise when participating in political conversations, attending pride parades, or otherwise choosing to show that non-LGBT+ people also support LGBT+ people, it is also worth examining if there are times when you may want to self-identify so that you are not mistaken for an LGBT+ person. This leads back to the self-conversation of where the line of activism and support is for you.

Now that you have considered the above areas for yourself, within your relationship, within your family, and within your professional capacity, it is also important to identify ways in which it is possible to do better and to do more. Although there may be more LGBT+ representation in the media than ever before, the number of LGBT+ hate crimes that occur each year continues to grow. But this is a statistic that can be reversed with increased career of diversity and inclusion, which can lead to acceptance and lower experiences of violence.

One way to improve is to listen to your LGBT+ employees and your LGBT+ colleagues. Being willing to hear the stories of LGBT+ people without interrupting them or turning the conversation back to you and your experiences allows that person to share their story and to feel heard as it is happening. While typical discussions are often a bit of a volley between participants listening and then sharing, specifically sharing experiences related to an LGBT+ identity can be very scary, especially for your newer employees, who may be trying to discern whether or not you are a safe person they can trust. If a person decides to share with you, understand that they are trusting you with something significant. This is not meant to be the same sort of conversation as if you were discussing favorite bands; it is instead a way that you are being asked to absorb and take in their experience.

Next, learn from those lessons being shared, knowing that your LGBT+ employees and LGBT+ colleagues are telling you something important. While it is common for people in majority groups to place the blame of negative interactions on minority members, listening to these stories can result in better understanding of how and why people are victimized. As is the case in any attack or victimization, it is never the victim's fault. It is never appropriate to ask a person why they didn't behave differently; it is instead necessary to validate that you have heard what they've shared, that you acknowledge their trust in you with a vulnerable part of themselves, and that you do not turn it into an opportunity to blame the victim for what someone else did to them.

Next, talk about it with others without outing the employee or colleague. When you are talking with others about the issues and stigma that LGBT+ people face, be sure to keep the stories that you tell of other people's lives vague enough so that you are not outing those who shared with you to new people. You can start with "I have an employee who…" or "I heard about a leader at another medical who…" If the details of the story are something, you find necessary to be heard by others, discuss this with the person who shared with you. Ask them if they would be open to sharing their story. Offer to go with them and sit by them if they agree to share their story. Or, if they are unwilling or unable, ask them if they would help you figure out what part of the story they would feel comfortable with you sharing. This allows them to remain in control of their own experiences, their personal stories, and their own truth. Once you have received the information and experience that an LGBT+ person has shared with you, think about how you can use this new knowledge to help bring about more inclusion and better resolutions to minimize safety concerns.

Finally, donate your time and your support to your LGBT+ employees and colleagues. Find ways to use the resources that you have to support inclusive policies and supportive programming. This may be by offering to mentor an LGBT+ employee directly, by introducing an LGBT+ colleague to someone in your professional network who may be of help to their goals, or by talking with your workplace about what they can do to create more opportunities for LGBT+ employees to be groomed for leadership roles. (This is not to give LGBT+ people an unfair advantage, it is just much more likely for these situations to occur organically in majority groups and much less likely to occur in marginalized groups without intentional effort.)

Chapter 4

Privilege

There has been a lot of discussion and debate about what privilege means, both as a term and how it impacts an individual's life. In reality, almost all of us have some modicum of privilege, whether overt or not. In fact, nearly all of us also have some situations in which we lack privilege. The point of acknowledging privilege is not to put down people who were or were not born a certain way or to blame people with privilege for having it. It is simply meant to lead to mindfulness. This allows a person to recognize the ways in which they benefit, which may not be something they regularly (or ever) consider.

What Counts as Privilege?

Anything that you get the benefit of that others do not counts as privilege. For example, if you can walk, talk, see, breathe, and eat on your own, you have privilege(s). If you live where there is not a war currently occurring, if you were taught to read, if you have access to sanitary supplies (including tampons/pads, toilet paper, and soap), and clean water, you have privilege(s). If, in television and films, you see couples and love stories of people of your gender and the gender of people you are attracted to, there is privilege. If you identify as the gender that matches your genitalia, there is privilege. If you are young or classically attractive or financially stable or well-fed or have air conditioning in your home or have a working vehicle or have access to medication when you are unwell or own books or watch television or have a smartphone or know how to drive or have a choice of clothing in your closet or if you sleep in a comfortable bed or consistently have electricity or bathe in warm water or have a consistent address, those are all privileges. In a world where COVID has existed, it is also a privilege to have either not had COVID or to have had it with mild symptoms (vs. long-COVID), to have had it at a time when loved ones could be with you for support, to have had access to vaccinations/boosters, to know there will be a ventilator for you if you need one, to

DOI: 10.4324/9781003167303-5

have had it late enough in the process that professionals know what it is and how to treat it, and even being able to die without being alone. So many did not experience these situations and it has led us to now add these details and opportunities to our list of medical privileges. As we consider the mental health side, we must recognize the lessened anxieties that come with knowing we have access to these treatments and supportive measures and that there is privilege in having not lost anyone to COVID as well.

Why Does Privilege Matter?

Too often, a conversation about privilege becomes an argument over who has more privilege than whom, which privilege is better to have than which other privilege, or what negative experiences counteract which privileges. This makes sense because it can be easy to assume that recognizing having privilege would be the same as claiming to have no problems or no right to complain about having problems. That's simply unrealistic and it can certainly inflame a conversation quite quickly. However, recognizing our privileges can help us to become more mindful of those who do not have what we have, as well as helping to articulate our needs to those who have what we do not.

For example, by recognizing that not everyone in your medical facility's location's community has consistent food access, a medical professional or staff member may become more aware of areas where wasted cafeteria food could be donated to those in need who may otherwise miss meals at home. By recognizing that the medical professional may have not yet experienced a lawsuit by an LGBT+ employee for discrimination and your company having not yet been in the news for noninclusive practices and policies means that the medical professional can begin to examine areas in which improvement is needed. There is now an opportunity to make these changes before and/or without creating conflict or experiencing legal ramifications because of the poor experience of an LGBT+ person.

In short, the purpose of defining one's privilege as an individual, as a department, as a medical, or as a medical community is not to belittle or undermine occurring problems or stressors. It is simply to examine the ways in which the existing structure and schema benefit some while being detrimental to others. Once this awareness is obtained, it can be easy to begin to assess where there are areas that can be improved upon, which can lead to change, and which in turn can lead to a more inclusive and affirming medical for all.

Chapter 5

Intersectionality

Although the definition section is intended to be all-encompassing, it seems inappropriate not to provide a separate place to discuss and recognize intersectionality. Coined by Kimberlé Williams Crenshaw in 1989, the term identifies the intersection of being a member of more than one minority group. It recognizes that each group's membership comes with its own struggles and that the intersection of two or more memberships is more than simply the sum of society's mistreatment of each group within which a person identifies. The definition in this context is acknowledging that although an LGBT+ identity is, in itself, a minority status, many individuals exist within the intersection of two or more minority groups, which directly impacts their medical experiences.

As one can imagine, each group that they are a part of causes them to be the target of misunderstanding and injustice, and to be at a higher risk of being victimized. The comic Wanda Sykes has built this into many of her comedy routines and interviews she has given, as she identifies as female, Black, and a lesbian. Her appearance allows the general public to assume her to be female and to identify her skin tone, leaving her already in a minority group at the intersection of female and Black. This individual exists at the intersection of female and Black and gay, creating three ways in which others may be biased against her, further causing her and others with this shared intersectionality to be that much more discriminated against than someone with only one of those three minority statuses, which is more discrimination than someone without any of these minority statuses faces.

In some cases, the identity of intersectionality may appear obvious. In other cases, there may be minority group status that may be more difficult for the casual observer to identify. In addition, there may be an assumption that certain members of certain minority groups may not identify as LGBT+. Typically, this occurs when one or more minority identifications lead the individual to be desexualized by society. One example of desexualized or infantilized groups is that of people with significant physical and/or learning disabilities. Through media portrayal and the additional need of assistance to perform daily tasks, it is common for society

DOI: 10.4324/9781003167303-6

to see individuals with physical limitations as patients, as helpless, and/or as people to be pitied. This makes it difficult for many to recognize any gender identity or sexual orientation in association with that individual or an entire group of individuals with the same characteristics. This can result in a lack of representation for LGBT+ individuals who have obvious physical limitations. The deaf community is another group where members are often not considered to also be in a gender or sexual minority. While our society has been making strides to recognize that hard-of-hearing or deaf people live rich, full lives, it remains prevalent in the media that individuals of this minority group are seen as being in need of assistance or being victims of crimes.

Although this book focuses on making medical facilities more LGBT+ inclusive, this is not intended to be done at the detriment of recognition of other minority groups or their needs. Focusing on this particular group and its needs can also provide you with insights and tools to become more mindful of the needs of patients, employees, and staff who are part of other minority groups. Use what you gain via this book to encourage you to think about how different employees may need similar types of support and how you can be a more inclusive provider and colleague.

Chapter 6

Battle Fatigue

As you move through this book, giving yourself time to pause periodically and reflect, you are encouraged to consider not just how the information impacts your life and your actions but also how the lack of knowledge and the need to educate others has impacted LGBT+ patients, patients' families, employees, colleagues, and community leaders. Too often, a person in a minority group is expected to provide insights to others. There can be an expectation that it is incumbent upon a person in a persecuted group to raise their hand, explain their identity, explain how the current statement or situation is inappropriate, offer suggestions, recommend a solution, and implement the new course of action.

It is also necessary to consider that laws and law enforcement may already be against them. (This is not to discount areas where nondiscrimination policies exist or the many wonderful police officers; this is simply to acknowledge how many areas of the nation lack even basic LGBT+ protections and how many stories exist where officers have been unkind or downright cruel to LGBT+ people.) There is also a significant amount of bigotry that exists, especially for those whose identities are at the intersection of a number of minority groups. This means that there may never be a time when the individual is able to truly relax because they are forced to always be in fear for their safety and their lives, spending a significant portion of their energy simply trying to stay alive, before they can even begin to add other areas of focus to their day.

As such, it is easy for a person to become exhausted from trying to meet or manage the expectations others have of them, while being seen as the voice of their entire minority group and while trying to avoid becoming the victim of violence. For LGBT+ employees, their jobs become that much more difficult when they are not only at risk as people but even more so in areas where it is legal for them to be fired for their identity, which means that they consistently also live in fear of sudden job and income loss.

Supportive close professional friends, direct supervisors, and team members of LGBT+ people may also experience this fatigue. This is because may be forced to

DOI: 10.4324/9781003167303-7

forever defend their person's identity to adults to ensure appropriate career opportunities and treatment in medical facilities, monitoring whether their sibling is safe from bullying or fending off those who mistreat them. This can result in significant and ongoing efforts by everyone to keep the LGBT+ person as safe and respected as possible.

As you move through this book and as you become more mindful of the experiences of LGBT+ people, you are encouraged to take time to think about when you personally have felt most unsafe, in danger, or at risk of violence. You are asked to think about how it felt when you were called down to the boss's office. You are asked to think about how your life would change if you were to be suddenly fired at this very moment. How would each of these situations feel?

As you consider each of these and the impact they would have on your life, you are encouraged to imagine the experience of living full-time in that feeling. You are asked to then consider how much additional strength it would take to feel this way and then complete your daily tasks and meet the expectations given to you by others. Finally, consider how it might feel if there was a person you could spend time with and a place you could go where those fears were lifted, where your safety was affirmed, and where your goals were supported. This is where you can begin to understand just how much of an impact you, your office, your medical, and your medical community can have on LGBT+ potential future employees, LGBT+ current employees, and LGBT+ colleagues.

Chapter 7

Terminology

As we get ready to begin, people may be on very different levels of understanding about the topics of this book. Additionally, some people believe they understand more than they do, and others probably understand more than they think they do. In a desire for everyone to begin on the same page, let's start off talking about terminology so that we all move forward together through the rest of the book.

Before we begin with current knowledge, let's take a moment to discuss the history of the naming of this group of people. We used to see the abbreviation that is GLBT (gay, lesbian, bisexual, and transgender); now we typically see it as LGBT+ (lesbian, gay, bisexual, and transgender). Why? Many women's groups argue that GLBT is yet another place where men are placed before women, so it is often considered more inclusive to place "lesbian" before "gay" as in "LGBT." However, as society and science begin to indicate that gender and sexuality may be more of a spectrum than a set number of boxes a person may check, it is becoming more common to see it listed as LGBT+. That allows for keeping the acronym short while also being the most inclusive possible.

All major medical and mental health professional organizations have long determined that inclusion, acceptance, and affirmation is what is best for LGBT+ people's health. This is really crucial because it considers the awareness that the LGBT+ population exists and why it exists, based on fact and on medical research. Too often, when talking about this population, there is an expectation that people's opinions should dictate how others are perceived. Instead, however, it is vital that we consider what professional associations say about this area in order to ensure that we are behaving based on best practices from science and research, rather than our own personal opinions, biases, or beliefs. (This is not to say that we can't acknowledge that we have our own opinions, biases, and beliefs; it is simply to indicate that although we have those, it is not our place as medical leaders to impose them on others.)

When looking at this from a leader perspective, we have to consider the ways in which our own personal behavior toward the treatment of those who identify as LGBT+ may be hindering their ability to learn and fully contribute to the academic community of our medical facility, medical community, and overall community.

DOI: 10.4324/9781003167303-8

Let's look at appropriate terminology. This is something that does change often, so you may see some terms that used to not be accepted now being used, and you may also see that some terms that used to be accepted no longer are. Let's start with the umbrella terms first and then work into what falls under those umbrellas.

In Broad Terms

<u>Sexual orientation:</u> This refers to someone's sexual and romantic attraction. Most people have a sexual orientation. (Someone who does not is called asexual.) You can be attracted (romantically, emotionally, and/or sexually) to people of the opposite gender and identify as "straight" or "heterosexual," or be attracted to people of the same gender and identify as "gay" or "lesbian." You can also be attracted to people of either gender, which is called "bisexual." Some people identify as being attracted to a person regardless of their gender. This person would identify as "pansexual." Some people question whether a sexual experience is required for a person to know their orientation. Although each individual is unique, there are plenty of people who identify their sexual orientation based on the feelings that they have, even if they have not had actual physical contact of a sexual nature.

<u>Gender identity:</u> Gender identity refers to a person's internal sense of being male, female, somewhere in between, or somewhere completely outside of the gender binary. For many people, one's gender identity corresponds with their biological facts; in other words, a person has female genitalia, and female DNA, and they identify as female. That makes the person cisgender. On the other hand, a person who identifies as transgender is someone who has external genitalia and DNA that do not match how that person sees themselves and how they identify in the world.

<u>Gender expression:</u> Gender expression relates to how a person chooses to communicate their gender identity to others through their clothing, hairstyles, manners, and behaviors. This may be conscious or subconscious. While most people's understanding of gender expression relates to masculinity and femininity, the expressions of these can occur in a myriad of ways, typically related to the impact of product marketing, mass media, and gender norms that date back generations. This is why we identify things like lace and glitter as being feminine and things like leather as being more masculine. Some people may choose an item specifically to broadcast their gender identity, and others may choose it because they enjoy it or like the way it feels, even if it does not necessarily correlate with their gender identity.

To summarize, sexual orientation describes who you feel sexually/romantically/emotionally attracted to. Gender identity is the gender that you feel in your brain regardless of your genitalia. Gender expression is what clothing, hairstyle, and mannerisms your conscious or subconscious mind chooses when you present yourself to the world.

Before we dive into the terminology under these umbrellas, let's look at the experience of someone coming out and then we'll dive into what the words mean that someone may come out as.

Chapter 8

Masking and Coming Out

Masking

In society, there is so much stigma, prejudice, and judgment about LGBT+ people that some hide their identity either from the world overall or from specific people. They may become intentional about their mannerisms, their choice of hairstyle, their attire, their career, their voice tone, and any other aspect of their identity that may make them seem LGBT+. This act of hiding one's self by following the expectations of society is called masking. When a person does come out (a process we'll break down in a moment), it is common to begin to see a distinct change in some or all aspects of how they present. This is because they are no longer hiding who they are behind this mask of heterosexuality or cisgender identity. For example, you may wonder why a neighbor comes out as gay and then suddenly begins to wear very different fashion or have a very different voice tone. Some mistakenly accuse the person of pretending to be their new identity. What you are actually witnessing is who that person is and always has been. They are simply no longer hiding behind a mask/façade in order to hide their identity from you.

Coming Out

What does "coming out" or "coming out of the closet" mean? It is the process of telling another person that you are LGBT+. There has been talk for decades about famous people coming out. Celebrities do it on the covers of magazines, singers do it at concerts or via their music videos, and some social media stars post entire videos of themselves coming out to their loved ones. In many areas of the country, the expectation is that of an immediate happy moment; an LGBT+ person hesitantly and fearfully tells someone they care about, and the person immediately embraces them and talks about how love knows no limits. In fact, it can be seen as homophobic/biphobic/transphobic if the person reacts any other way. While there is a lot

DOI: 10.4324/9781003167303-9

to unpack in terms of the coming-out experience within families, let's focus on the experience and its importance within a medical setting.

When a person comes out at any age, they are choosing to let their medical provider(s) know something very personal about them. In addition, if an employee comes out to you, this can be a surprise, and that surprise can lead to an uncomfortable or awkward interaction. As such, it can be better for medical providers and staff to think through the process generally, so they are at least somewhat prepared when the situation occurs in the future, whether with a patient or a colleague.

If a Patient or Colleague Comes Out to You

It is important to keep the focus on the person coming out. Your personal thoughts, feelings, or opinions about LGBT+ people, coming out, or that patient or employee are not relevant in that moment. Instead, be mindful that the person is trusting you with information that speaks to their identity. Patients are vulnerable in that they have come to you as a person of medical authority, respect that impact on top of the personal information they have just shared with you. Interns and employees at the lowest positions in your company are growing and developing into future industry leaders, and their sense of self and sense of self-worth is very malleable at this time. Your reaction and response can help or hinder their mental health and their self-confidence. No matter who is coming out to you, you may choose to thank them for sharing this. If the person is coming out as a different gender, it may be appropriate to ask them if they would like you to call them by another name or use different pronouns. You might also wish to let them know that you accept them and that they can come to you any time they are in need of support.

You may want to inquire into who else knows. Here, you may glean information about whether the news is common knowledge among their support network, whether they have chosen to share this information with others, and how their home life is going. Remember that, unless there is a safety concern, it is never your place or your right to share this information with others. This is not a silly personality quirk that is fair game to joke about with the employee; this is not gossip for the break room; this is not a topic to discuss at a nurses' station. Employee safety and privacy must be a priority, especially in a situation where sharing this information can lead to discrimination, bullying, or self-harm. If you think the employee may be at risk of being harmed or harming themselves, follow standard safety protocols. However, be sure to find out beforehand whether the person or people who are involved in creating these protocols (those in the Human Resources department or those in any Employee Assistance Program offered) are affirming and accepting. You want to guide the employee to get the help they need; you do not want to refer them to someone who will further the problem. If you find that there is no one in that position to refer the employee to, reach out to a state or national hotline for LGBT+ issues, and they can guide you toward the best option for employee safety in this situation. Patient safety is perhaps even more critical and must be protected at equal levels of importance as employee care.

Also, allow the person coming out to guide the conversation and to end it when they feel they are done sharing. You can periodically check in with them privately and keep an extra eye out for any struggles they may be having by asking them how they are doing. However, your treatment of the employee or patient should otherwise not change from before they came out to you. The goal is not to treat them as either less or more than others; it is simply to ensure their safety and to be an affirming person for them within the context of your interactions.

Although it is common for the assumption to be that coming out is a stressor only for developing adults whose peers can be rude or downright cruel, the coming-out experience for anyone of any age can also be stressful. Coming out to a work colleague or medical provider can be even more anxiety-inducing. Although there are legal protections to keep a person from being fired for being LGBT+ and from discrimination by a medical care provider, this does not mean that every medical facility is accepting, affirming, or kind to LGBT+ people. As a result, their letting you know something personal can feel like opening the door to be judged, ridiculed, or mistreated. It is vital that you respond with kindness and support.

If Someone Who Reports to You Comes Out to You

Let the staff member know that you value them, and you appreciate their choice to trust you with this information. If they are alerting you to a difference in gender identity, ask if they would like you to call them by another name or to use different pronouns. You can also ask for additional guidance on how you can best support them. Just as with employees coming out, this information is highly personal and should never be discussed with others unless a safety concern is present. If there is such a concern, find out the protocol set up by your medical facility. In many cases, there is an employee assistance program hotline you can call with questions. Be sure to keep the colleague's name anonymous while researching how to help, in order to protect their privacy. Just as with an employee situation, if you are unsure whether a referral is to someone accepting, reach out to a state or federal LGBT+ help hotline for guidance.

Chapter 9

More Terminology

Now that we've covered the overarching umbrella terminology and the coming out experience, let's look at the terminology under these umbrellas so you can better understand what the identity words are that someone may have used when they came out publicly or to you.

Sexual Orientations

Gay: A man who is romantically and sexually attracted to other males. This may also be used as a term that is more inclusive which would encompass gay men, lesbians, and people who identify as bisexual.

Lesbian: A woman whose romantic and sexual attraction is to other women.

Bisexual: A person who is sexually/romantically/emotionally attracted to both men and women, though not necessarily simultaneously. A bisexual person may not be attracted equally to both genders, and the degree of attraction may change over time.

Pansexual: A person who is sexually/romantically/emotionally attracted to a person of any gender identity.

A common expression is "hearts not parts" because their attraction is to the person's heart and emotions, not at all dependent on the genitalia or body parts the person may or may not have.

Asexual: A person who has no sexual or romantic attraction. This is not due to the person having a medication side effect or no longer being interested in their spouse/partner, they simply do not feel this urge.

DOI: 10.4324/9781003167303-10

> Medically, it is important to ask questions about this only when assessing first if this is a problem for the patient/client and, if so, to tell whether this is tied to recent changes in medication, relationship, or hormones versus something that has always been.

Lesbians

It should not be assumed that lesbians have never been sexually active with men; we cannot assume when talking with employees that they have not had sexual encounters with males. Making this assumption can leave them unsafe due to lack of information given, because there is an assumption that information is not useful. The risks of suicidal ideation, self-harm, and depression may be higher in lesbians and bisexual individuals, especially those who are not open about their sexual orientation, who are not in satisfying and safe relationships, and/or who lack social support. Smoking and obesity rates are also higher in lesbians and bisexual women because smoking and eating are inexpensive ways in which some cope, and this population may be more likely to need coping mechanisms to deal with the stress of living in a world that is often homophobic and biphobic.

In addition, many lesbian and bisexual women are victims of hate crimes, and they often fear for their safety. Intimate partner violence may also occur between women in same-sex relationships at a rate that is similar to heterosexual relationships. Lesbian women can also be raped, physically assaulted, or stalked by a female partner. It may be difficult for employees to be open about this, especially if they do not feel supported at home and within the medical community. They may struggle with addressing these concerns and their relationships out of fear that they will not be believed, or that people will assume that women cannot be as violent toward each other as men have been known to be violent in interactions with women. If an employee comes to you with concerns about relationship safety, it is necessary that you follow the same protocol the medical facility has for opposite-sex relationships and for any report of violence whatsoever.

Gay and MSM

This categorizes male-identified people who have sexual encounters and/or relationship with other male-identified people. At the present time, some see "gay" as an identity that deals with a specific type of personality or type of behavior. In those cases, some do not identify as "gay" but rather as "MSM"—men who have sex with men. (This may be how a male-identified employee or patient identifies his sexuality, even if his age and/or appearance do not yet make him a "man" by definition. This may also be because the individual man separates being part of the gay community from whom he has sex with, causing him to identify as not a member of the gay community though he is still engaging in sex with one or more men.)

Regardless of a person's chosen label, there is still an increased risk for this population of sexually transmitted infections (STIs) as well as psychological and behavioral disorders related to their experiences and whether or not they are accepted at home. It may be easy to find statistics that indicate that gay men or men who have sex with men are contracting more STIs than other groups; however, this research is often heavily biased either in the way the study was written to bolster preexisting misperceptions or by misinterpreting the results to further a person or group's agenda, regardless of the breadth of research that indicates otherwise.

This may be because the people funding the study have personal or religious feelings about homosexuality. It may be because a drug company is biased in their studies in an attempt to indicate a need for a drug they are trying to sell. It may also be that the place in which these studies occur is heavily biased toward or against one type or group of people. For example, doing a study while inside a nightclub will likely only capture the responses of people who go to nightclubs; it will not also include people who do not go to nightclubs, which may be a significantly different experience. This detail is important to know so that you can both consider your own biases and beliefs and have an understanding that parents of employees may make assumptions based on biased research that can cause them to be not accepting and not affirming of their employees. With this in mind, homosexuality has been associated with a higher risk of psychological and behavioral disorders, including depression, anxiety disorders, suicidal thoughts and plans, eating disorders, alcohol and substance abuse, and cigarette smoking. The stigmatization of homosexuality in American society results in the frequent exposure of homosexual men to discrimination and victimization. This is believed to be a causative factor in the development of psychological and behavioral disorders.

Bisexual and Pansexual

In bisexual and pansexual people, it is a common misconception that a person who identifies as one of these is either "greedy" or uncertain. Others believe that a person identified as bisexual or pansexual is actually gay, but they are not yet ready to admit that. This is inaccurate. There has been no single pattern to prove this assumption. Some people in these groups feel they fit into neither the heterosexual nor homosexual world, while others feel identified more predominantly as being attracted to one gender identity than the other. Due to a lack of understanding, acceptance, or even knowledge of these identities, the failing relationship issues facing these people seldom emerge when contemplating policy and legal changes. Some people have legally married opposite-sex partners. As a result, they are able to access the privileges afforded to married couples. However, many people are not married. They may choose not to get married, or their family may not be accepting of their union. Some may wish to become parents regardless of their marital status. Bisexual and pansexual people often face similar discrimination and obstacles to those faced by gay and lesbian people in regard to custody, visitation, or adoption of employees. This means that in addition to your employees possibly identifying as bisexual or pansexual, you may have employees who are dealing with parents who identify as lesbian, gay, bisexual, or transgender.

Not only is this something employees are learning about as they become clearer in their own sexuality, but this may also be impacting the custody agreements about them if the parents have already been divorced, or it may lead to parents being divorced. It is necessary to be respectful of this and to be mindful that this may be an aspect of the employee's personal life which may impact their behaviors and their abilities in the office, not because they do not care or because they are too lazy to complete their work, but because they may have these trials going on at home which may be too much of a distraction and emotional burden to manage while being able to complete all tasks on time.

Greysexual and Asexual

Greysexual is the limited capacity or low-level impact of sexual desire. This does not mean that the person does not or cannot feel romantically attracted to someone or that they are unable to build an emotional or intellectual connection with them. It simply means that they do not feel a significant or strong desire for sexual connection. Some still engage in sexual behaviors as they may see this as a compromise they make for a partner they love or they may be interested in engaging in these behaviors very infrequently. However, this is not something that motivates them.

Asexuality is the absence of sexual desire. The person may identify as "ace." This does not mean that the person does not or cannot feel romantically attracted to someone or that they are unable to build an emotional or intellectual connection with them. It simply means that they do not feel a desire for sexual connection. Some still engage in sexual behaviors as they may see this as a compromise they make for a partner they love. However, this is not something that motivates them.

Autisexual

This term is newer as the research is still growing in recognizing a connection between LGBT+ people and those who have an autism diagnosis. It is an identity with a basis that states that this sexual and/or gender identity can only be understood in the context of being autistic, when one's autism greatly affects one's sexuality.[1-2]

Gender Identity

People generally experience gender identity and sexual orientation as two different things. Sexual orientation refers to one's sexual attraction to others, whereas gender identifies a reference to one's sense of oneself in their own identity. Usually, the gender that the individual is attracted to does not change when a person begins to live openly as a transgender person. For example, a person assigned male at birth who is attracted to women will be attracted to women after transitioning, when they openly identify as female. This will mean that this person who was once seen by society as a heterosexual man would now be seen by the world as a lesbian.

Let's talk about gender! In present-day American society, there is an overarching norm that gender is binary—that is, that there are two options (male or female). This is decided based on external genitalia.

> This is what is announced at "gender reveal parties," as it is based on whether the fetus does or does not have a penis. Sex and gender are not the same thing. Sex is the chromosomal designation of a person's genetics, whereas gender is a social construct. In other words, it should be called a "sex reveal party," since no one will know how the staff member identifies their gender for some time yet!

How is gender guided by society? This begins before a person is even born. It includes when people ask whether the baby is a boy or a girl. It includes when parents begin to envision their person's future extra-curricular activities (football or ballet, fixing cars or going shopping). It is often used to decide themes for baby showers, to send baby gifts, and to decorate nurseries. Pink and lace for girls; blue and trucks for boys. Check out the baby and staff member aisles in stores and you'll see this on full display: lace and ruffles for girls, reinforced knees on pants for boys. Hair and makeup toys in pink packages for girls; wrestling action figures and superheroes in blue packages for boys. In the tween and teen sections of stores, girls' areas are often filled with sparkly jewelry, whereas boys' sections have items meant not to stain easily. Everywhere you look, society shows that girls must be petite, delicate, and appearance-based, and boys are meant to be rough and tumble. While this may not be news to you, have you ever considered that society is also showing that there are only two genders?

What is gender? Gender is the way a person identifies their place in a spectrum of masculine and feminine, or outside of that spectrum altogether. How do people identify themselves within this spectrum?

Transgender

A broad term meaning that a person's gender identity does not match their assigned gender at birth. In other words, their identity does not match either their external genitalia and sex characteristics and/or their chromosomal sex.

Cisgender

A term to describe a person whose gender identity does match their assigned gender at birth. This means that transgender and cisgender are opposite terms.

Gender Nonbinary

A term to describe a person who identifies as a gender that is not male or female but may be a combination of the two or something different. (You may hear this abbreviated as "NB" and/or see this abbreviated in writing as "enby"—the phonetic pronunciation of NB. As the abbreviation of "NB" has long been in use in communities of color to indicate "non-Black," "enby" is the most inclusive written form of abbreviation for nonbinary.)

Gender Fluid

A term to describe a person whose gender identity may change or evolve over time. This goes beyond a desire to wear a dress one day and pants the next, as this is not about gender expression and clothing or hairstyle but rather about the identity of a person and how they are in their gender from day to day.

> Former Nike employee and athlete Renee (Ron) Roley once described this as thinking of gender like a lava lamp; it fluctuates differently over time and for each person.

Neurogender

Neurogender is a gender feeling that is linked to someone's neurodivergence. It can be both an identity and an umbrella term for genders that are limited to neurodivergent people. Obviously, you have to be neurodivergent to identify as this gender as it means that a person's perception of their gender is influenced by them being neurodivergent.[3]

Agender

A term to describe a person who does not identify as having a gender.

These identities are also why we have added the + to the LGBT+ in our language, and why you will typically see more recent publications or speeches referring to this population as LGBT+.

> *Note:* Transgender, cisgender, gender nonbinary, gender fluid, neurogender, and agender are adjectives, not nouns. Just like Black, Asian, Hispanic, short, and tall. There is no such word as "transgendered," as the word is not a verb, so it cannot have a past tense. Always put the word "person" after the gender-identifying word, as this is a word to describe someone. This is just the way you don't see a "short," you see a "short person." You may see the term "male

to female transgender person" or "female to male transgender person." This has been used for quite some time to first identify the person's gender assigned at birth and second identify the gender the person identifies as. For example, a "male to female transgender person" would indicate that the person was assumed by others to be a male person at birth (due to external genitalia) and now identifies and/or lives as a female person.

However, updated terminology has also caused some to redefine the categorization of transgender people because science is indicating that gender is being seen more and more as a social construct. This would mean that nobody is born with a gender, since nobody is born with an innate sense of social construct. With that in mind, the terminology is being changed. Now, the identity of a transgender person is typically described as "assigned female at birth" (AFAB) or "assigned male at birth" (AMAB).

Medical options for transgender people: This is a conversation that is necessary because medical leaders may see the results of some of these different actions and choices in the transgender population within their medical facility, whether with an employee, staff member, or parent in the medical's community.

Some mistakenly believe that medical options are easily acquired and happen quickly. In America, to be able to receive any medical intervention, the person must typically be consistently seen by a licensed mental health professional for many months or years, working in concert with a medical professional or team before any medical interventions can occur. In addition, health insurances do not typically cover any of these interventions, so many families spend years saving money to afford what is best for the individual. This means that although something may seem sudden to you, by the time you are aware of the change, the family and individual have likely spent years being guided by multiple health-care professionals. No one takes this lightly, and no medical interventions are offered or are an option until/unless multiple specifically trained gender professionals have done their work to ensure that this is the appropriate treatment for the person.

Not all transitions look the same.

This will come up again when having conversations later in this book about restrooms and other ways in which employees and leaders should be mindful so that transitioning employees are not discriminated against intentionally or accidentally.

Some may have transitioned from a young age:

A young patient or the child of an employee or staff member may be in the process of deciding if or when to begin puberty blockers. This is a type of medication that prevents the body from beginning adult puberty. This means that people assigned male at birth will not grow facial and body hair, their voice will not deepen, and their genitals will not grow. For a person assigned male at birth who identifies as female, this is vital. If not given puberty blockers, a person identifying as a girl would have to watch her body become increasingly more male in appearance. This can create extreme anxiety and depression. It may even result in suicide attempts. For people assigned female at birth, puberty blockers prevent the body shape from changing at a time when hips would become wider and breasts would begin to grow. This can make a person who identifies as male become incredibly uncomfortable and feel unsafe in a body that is growing increasingly dissimilar to their gender identity. It can be a very unsafe time for a transgender young person if puberty blockers are not provided. There have long been assumptions or fears that youth who begin these blockers will have regrets or will not choose to continue these once they become adults who have legal control over their medical care. This aligns with assumptions that parents force their children into identities that are not actually who the child is. However, research proves this assumption to be both factually inaccurate and incredibly harmful. A 2022 study by The Gender Identity Clinic of the Amsterdam UMC Hospital Center in the Netherlands studied adolescent patients who had been diagnosed with gender dysphoria and prescribed puberty blockers. Of the cohort, 98% reported continued use of hormone replacement therapy in a follow-up after starting.[4]

"To our knowledge, this study is the first to assess continuation of gender-affirming hormones in a large group of transgender individuals who started medical treatment with puberty suppression in adolescence," the study said. "The key message [of the study] is that the majority of people, who went through a thorough diagnostic evaluation prior to starting treatment, continued gender-affirming hormones at follow-up," Dr. Marianne van der Loos, a physician at Amsterdam UMC and a co-author of the study said, "This is reassuring regarding the recent increased public concern about regret of transition." This comes as leading health-care organizations there—including the Texas Medical Association and Texas Pediatric Society[5]—have stated that gender-affirming care is the best way to provide for the needs of trans youth. Other national organizations, such as the American Psychiatric Association[6] among others, have expressed similar support. Kathryn Lowe, MD, FAAP, a member of the American Academy of Pediatrics Section on Lesbian, Gay, Bisexual, Transgender Health and Wellness Executive Committee, became an advocate for transgender children in Montana after witnessing a youth who transitioned about 6 years ago. "It was an incredible experience to watch her truly blossom and come to life her parents understood that she was transgender and allowed her to transition and live as her authentic self," she said. "Seeing this (individual) go from struggling with depression and anxiety to being a happy thriving child is what inspired me to do all I can to support gender diverse kids as well as work to help build a society that also supports and affirms gender-diverse kids." She speaks of the critical importance of medical professionals speaking up against bills that prevent gender-diverse children from receiving care deemed necessary by their families and care providers. New bills have been introduced, but Dr. Lowe said she has learned that she can make a difference. "Many of us pediatricians often are nervous to speak up or to pick up the phone," she said. "I really think the voice of pediatricians can be so powerful that many people really respect our voices … we are in a place to use our platform and our position to really make a difference in the lives of these vulnerable kids."[7]

The American Academy of Child and Adolescent Psychiatry (AACAP) has also taken a public stand, stating "Many reputable professional organizations, including the American Psychological Association, the American Psychiatric Association, the American Academy of Pediatrics, and the Endocrine Society, which represent tens of thousands of professionals across the United States, recognize natural variations in gender identity and expression and have published clinical guidance that promotes nondiscriminatory, supportive interventions for gender diverse youth based on the current evidence base. These interventions may include, and are not limited to, social gender transition, hormone blocking agents, hormone treatment, and affirmative psychotherapeutic modalities. The American Academy of Child and Adolescent Psychiatry (AACAP) supports the use of current evidence-based clinical care with minors. AACAP strongly opposes any efforts—legal, legislative, and otherwise—to block access to these recognized interventions. Blocking access to timely care has been shown to increase youths' risk for suicidal ideation and other negative mental health outcomes."[8]

Overall, this indicates a long-term, clear, scientific, research-based, consistently proven truth that health promotion for all youth encourages open exploration of all identity issues, including sexual orientation, gender identity, and/or gender expression according to recognized practice guidelines.[9,10] Research consistently demonstrates that gender diverse youth who are supported to live and/or explore the gender role that is consistent with their gender identity have better mental health outcomes than those who are not.[11,12,13] Yet until these protections become universal, children still worry and this worry can be overwhelming. The Trevor Project's 2022 study showed that "93% of transgender and nonbinary youth said that they have worried about transgender people being denied access to gender affirming medical care due to state or local laws."[14]

When transitioning begins, in addition to blocking the puberty hormones that are not congruent with gender identity, hormones will begin to be introduced that encourage the body to develop in a way that aligns with the person's identity. This means beginning testosterone for people assigned female at birth who identify as male. That testosterone will do what it does in cisgender male teenagers: it will cause the voice to deepen, facial, and body hair to begin to grow, and all other male physical characteristics to begin to develop. For people assigned male at birth, the hormone introduced is estrogen, which allows for a more feminine shape, the raising of the voice pitch, and for breasts to begin to grow. In situations in which youth identify as transgender before puberty and have affirming and supportive parents, the use of puberty blockers followed by gender-confirming hormones can result in a person that appears to the public to be the gender in which they identify, though their genitalia may not match. In situations in which the family and/or colleagues are not affirming, these individuals may become increasingly unsafe and this can increase the risk of self-harm or suicidality. Some may attempt to remove genitalia, and others may seek out illegal hormone blockers or hormone replacements in hopes of preventing their body from changing due to their natural hormones. In situations in which parents are not affirming, while hormone blockers and new hormones cannot simply be provided by the medical professionals at random, it will be necessary that medical leaders be very mindful of the mental health of these employees and work with them to make plans in order to ensure their safety and to find ways to prioritize patient care over their parents' refusal to provide care.

> Later, this book will guide you toward setting up a safer facility, as these individuals may struggle with being bullied by peers who are aware that they are transgender, even if the person presents as the gender in which they identify.

Although it is common that people are interested in this type of hormonal impact on someone, it is never ever okay to ask a person to disclose what hormones, if any, they may be taking. The only reason for this to be asked/known is if the human resources office or a medical insurance office is inquiring specifically to meet an individual's medical needs regarding insurance plans, or if the person chooses to volunteer this information. While it is normal and typical for people to be interested, especially those who lack insight into this process, it is not the patient's or employee's role to educate their colleagues or supervisors, nor their care providers. Instead, refer to this book and its resources to find out more without creating a situation in which the individual feels obligated to disclose or unsafe.

However, it is possible or even likely that among local or national or even international colleagues, there will be those who identify as transgender. They may have or may not have had any type of hormonal intervention or surgeries. This may include genital reconstruction surgery (typically referred to as gender confirmation surgery, though this terminology does change frequently); breast implants; the shaving down of an Adam's apple; a brow lift and shaving of the brow bone, or another surgery to feminize the face of a person assigned male at birth; or fat injections, breast reduction or chest reconstruction, and other options for people to appear more masculine for those assigned female at birth. Some identify a part of their body as not being congruent with their identity and thus want to make changes as quickly as medically possible. Others simply do not connect those aspects of their body to being related to gender the way that many do. At no time is it ever appropriate to ask about which surgeries, if any, a person has had. The only people who need to know that information are the person and their medical practitioners.

It should be noted that those who do undergo some form of surgery may have additional needs due to the reason for their surgery. While a cisgender woman having breast implants placed or removed is likely able to find a local specialist, have insurance cover costs (if it is not considered cosmetic), and have support during the healing process, this is not the same experience for many transgender people. A 2022 study found that 56% of patients who underwent feminizing genital surgery, a procedure known as vaginoplasty, and 50% of patients who underwent masculinizing genital surgery, or phalloplasty, had their procedure done outside their state of residence.

The findings also suggest that costs associated with patients' travels come with a substantial financial burden. Those who needed to have their care in a different state had to pay nearly 50% more in out-of-pocket medical expenses. "We already knew that traveling for health care requires patients to take time off work and pay for travel and lodging on their own, and that it can make receiving follow-up care from qualified providers who are familiar with each patient's unique needs challenging," said Jae Downing, the study's lead author and an assistant professor of health policy at Oregon Health and Science University. "Now, our study shows that traveling out of state also increases out-of-pocket medical expenses for trans and gender-diverse patients—even though their surgery's total cost is largely the same," they added.[15] As a result, if someone you know shares that they are planning or scheduling one of these surgeries, you may wish to consider the unique additional costs, time, and stress likely to be experienced by them.

Those whom you work with, from interns to CEOs from young patients to elder patients may be at any aspect of their transition. Do not make assumptions based on their age, on your location's laws, on the media, or on how the individual appears to you. As we have seen, not only do surgical choices depend on the individual's identity and body, these decisions are also often dependent on their financial ability to travel, miss work, and pay for recovery care. Much of this may be unaffordable and thus there may be substantial impact to the person's mental health and to their sense of self. Those who are able to undergo these affirming procedures may then require significant time to rebuild their paid time off, their bank accounts, and the like due to the impact had.

A transgender person is not "more trans" or "less trans" based on how far through a transition process the person is. Some people choose never to take hormones and never to have surgery, others only choose to utilize some of the treatment options, and others choose to alter their physical appearance without utilizing any hormonal or surgical options. This is a personal choice based on their own feelings about their bodies and based on financial options available.

Some people believe that they can identify a transgender person simply by looking at them. While this might have been largely true in past generations because there was no opportunity to utilize hormones and surgical options, the idea that this is an obvious identity is incredibly outdated, and the imagery that people use is incredibly biased. There are many people who identify as transgender, gender nonconforming, or gender nonbinary whose appearance may give no indication of their gender identity.

It is not their obligation to provide this information to you. You may have access to this information if the medical facility listed the patient or employee under one name and gender but the person presents and identifies differently. In these cases, make sure to communicate with your supervisor in order to make sure that the name and pronouns within the office for the person are what they have asked to be called. You may also wish to speak with your supervisor about changing the name and pronoun on the sign-in sheets, HR forms, and any computer programming in order to ensure that the person is not misgendered or misnamed in places where they or others consistently see this information. Remember that a transgender person is just like any other person; their body and their choices with their body are none of your business unless you are a medical professional treating them and the question you are asking is medically necessary. While you may have questions, it is not the individual's job to teach you nor is it appropriate for you to expect such. If, however, you are unsure, ask the person privately and follow their lead. Never ask a person of any age about this information or anything related to their identity in front of others. It is already very difficult for transgender people of all ages to avoid bullying or violence, and putting the spotlight on their identity in front of others may make the situation much harder for them.

Some associate the idea of a transgender person with being a drag queen. They're very, very different. Drag queens and drag kings are often biological males and females, respectively, who present as members of the other sex specifically to perform or entertain. The performance may include singing, lip-synching, or dancing. Drag performers may or may not identify as transgender. Many drag queens and kings identify as gay, lesbian, or bisexual. This is very different from a transgender person, whose heart and mind are of a gender that is different than their genitalia and who is living as themselves. Transgender people do not do this for the entertainment or amusement of others; it is simply who the person is. As an example, this is the difference between the way you may choose to dress up for Halloween and your identity every day; one is meant to be fun and entertaining, and the other simply is who you are.

While it used to be very rare for anybody to openly identify as LGBT+, the past decades have significantly changed this, though politically, this may depend on the area in which you live and/or work. Members of boy bands including members of New Kids on the Block and *NSYNC have come out as gay. Sonny and Cher's son has come out as a transgender man, living openly, and with the support of his parents. Top musicians have also identified themselves as bisexual, or lesbian, taking their partners with them to very public events. This can be incredibly helpful and affirming for those in the LGBT+ community; however, the social change of people feeling more able to be out and live openly does not mean that bullying does not happen. In order to prevent bullying in the medical and in general, allies are necessary.

Proof of Identity

When looking at estimates for how many LGBT+ people there are in any given city, state, or country, it is very difficult to accurately account for this. This is because there is often bias in the accounting experience, and it also requires a person not only to be out but also to trust the survey taker with this personal information. This can lead to statistics that are much lower than are actually accurate in terms of how many people identify as LGBT+ in America today.

This is often because statistics are tied into surveys, which can have skewed data based on the collection method and funding source, and to legal identification changes. The process of legally changing one's gender varies by state; however, some major agencies are changing their requirements and providing new options. In 2022, the federal government changed their policy on social security gender change. "The Social Security Administration's Equity Action Plan includes a commitment to decrease administrative burdens and ensure people who identify as gender diverse or transgender have options in the Social Security Number card application process," said Acting Commissioner Kijakazi. "This new policy allows people to self-select their sex in our records without needing to provide documentation of their sex designation." The press release then includes additional information on updates and on who is still not yet fully seen in the policy. "People who update their sex marker in Social Security's records will need to apply for a replacement SSN card. They will still need to show a current document to prove their identity, but they will no longer need to provide medical or legal documentation of their sex designation now that the policy change is in place.

The agency will accept the applicant's self-identified sex designation of either male or female, even if it is different from the sex designation shown on identity documents, such as a passport or state-issued driver's license or identity card. SSN cards do not include sex markers. Currently, Social Security's record systems are unable to include a nonbinary or unspecified sex designation. The agency is exploring possible future policy and systems updates to support an 'X' sex designation for the SSN card application process."[16]

The Department of Veteran Affairs has a similar policy now in place, as of January 2022. "All veterans, all people, have a basic right to be identified as they define themselves," VA Secretary Denis McDonough said in a statement. "This is essential for their general well-being and overall health. Knowing the gender identity of transgender and gender-diverse veterans helps us better serve them." In addition, "It also allows healthcare providers within the VA better understand the needs of their patients," he said. The VA last year began including gender identifiers in its medical record system, which now includes "transgender male," "transgender female," "nonbinary," "other," or "does not wish to disclose" options. The press release also stated "A person's gender identity conveys essential information about who they are and may signal experiences of stigma and discrimination that can affect their health. VA health records now display both gender identity and preferred name, so VA staff can address the Veteran appropriately."[17]

However, a provider should not assume that every person has a gender marker that aligns with their identity. Sometimes this is because states may have different requirements as proof of reason for the change while others may make it too expensive or time-consuming for many to endure. Those who are in the process of immigrating or those who are in process of being accepted into universities or those with major medical situations may not submit for legal name or gender changes due to the risk of paperwork or approval concerns. In addition, far too often, transgender and gender-variant kids are kicked out of their homes when they come out. (Family conflict about youths' LGBT+ identities was a factor in this housing instability, with 40% of youth who said they had been kicked out and 55% of youth who said they had run away or been abandoned reporting that it had been due to mistreatment or fear of mistreatment related to their LGBT+ identity.[18]) Plus, adults with these identities are less likely to be employed and paid fairly. [According to a 2019 Williams Institute analysis of Behavioral Risk Factor Surveillance System data, about one in five LGBT+ adults in the United States (22%) live in poverty. Furthermore, Black (40%) and Latinx (45%) transgender adults are more likely to live in poverty than transgender people of any other race.[19]] As a result of both, there are many who are unhoused. Without a permanent mailing address (and often without having their birth certificate and/or social security card), it can be impossible for a person to prove who they are and to obtain documents typically mailed many weeks after the forms are completed. This can lead to situations in which proving identity is more than difficult enough, leaving no opportunity for the completion of these gender-change processes.

When working with or caring for a transgender person, a few tips:

■ First, it isn't always about the person's transgender status. It is important not to focus so narrowly on the fact that a person is transgender that you end up making that characteristic more important than the actual reason the person is seeking your help or support or insight or guidance. It is important that you help them focus on the real issue and steer them away from focusing on their gender identity if that is not the core problem. For example, if a transgender intern is struggling with a medical question, it is important to focus on the question or to discuss how to better train the intern on the skills they need in order to do their job well. It would make sense in some cases to be mindful that the intern may have some additional struggles simultaneously due to their gender identity. However, it is also very likely that this is an employee simply struggling with topic, just the way so many cisgender interns do during their intern years. By focusing on internship and learning concerns, it allows the intern to be guided appropriately without ignoring the real issue of difficulty, and without letting the intern off the hook for making mistakes by lessening your expectations of their abilities due to their transgender identity.

■ Second, be aware of the assumptions you are making about a person's gender. It is very common to assume that you know a person's gender or gender identity based on stereotypes. Some people's expression or identity is not stereotypical and may be different from what you would expect or assume. Therefore, it is important to be open to allow a person to self-identify. If you are unsure, it is appropriate to ask the person how they would like to be addressed. Often, this can be taken care of easily on the first interaction. Just as when you meet a person for the first time and give them the opportunity to identify the name they prefer to be called, the same can be true for transgender people. Just as a person named Elizabeth would tell you on the first interaction that she prefers to be called Liz or Lizzie or Beth, it is equally appropriate for a person named David to tell you that she prefers to be called Denise. Just as you would make a note that Elizabeth has asked to be called Liz, you should do the same for a transgender person so that all people in your facility are spoken to and called by the name that they go by. This allows for inclusive offices without doing anything that singles out a transgender person. When thinking about employees, if you are in a decision-making position, you will also want to ensure that any e-mail address, nameplate on an office door/cubical, in the company directory, on staff name badges, and anywhere else where their name will be displayed.

■ It is also important to be mindful of orientation assumptions. While most people do identify as heterosexual, not all do. This means that if a person is talking about someone they are dating, do not assume that the person is speaking of someone of a different gender. Making these assumptions or making jokes in a conversation may seem light and fun but they could put a target on an individual who needs to lie about their life for their safety or may cause them to feel as if they are in an office where it may not be safe. Instead, you can simply remind all employees or patients that talking about their date on Friday night is not a conversation meant to be happening in the middle of your consultation or time together and encourage them to focus on why they are there, just as you would any other person talking about any other date.

■ It is also important to know the laws. This is a constantly changing situation. While this is not always something that everyone can keep up with, it may make sense in your medical facility for the supervisor or point person to assign one person whose job it is to be mindful of changes. This can create a protocol in which legal changes can be sent by e-mail to the entire staff so that everyone is aware. In addition, if you live in a state in which the laws are less than inclusive and respectful, this does not require you not to be inclusive or respectful. You can always curate a medical system, a medical building, and/or your office to be a place in which each person who comes through your doors can be authentically themselves.

■ Next, except in rare cases, it is very important that you use the name and the pronoun that corresponds to that person's gender identity. In addition, the person may choose to use a name that is gender-neutral or associated with the opposite gender for the pronoun; it is important to be aware of and respect this. This may mean that someone named Brian prefers to be called Brian but uses female pronouns. This may mean that your employee prefers to be called Sam—a name that does not distinguish their gender—just like Elizabeth prefers to be called Liz. Just like Elizabeth preferring to be called Liz, simply marking this in all documentations and, for employees, on all staff name badges and directories, reminds you always to call on them using the name they have asked to be called, showing respect to the individual.

Transgender-friendly policies in this book will discuss what that means, how to create them, and what to do if others in your medical facility are less welcoming.

As we move forward in this book, there may be situations that feel unrealistic because the people in your community are not inclusive, or those who explore related decisions are not inclusive. You are not being asked to go directly against what your supervisors say, but nothing prevents you from being someone who is aware of the knowledge and science related to the LGBT+ community. Nothing prevents you from being someone who is welcoming, and nothing prevents you from letting your employees know that homophobic, biphobic, and transphobic language is never okay in your office.

Notes

1 Cooper, K., Mandy, W., Butler, C., & Russell, A. (2023). Phenomenology of gender dysphoria in autism: A multiperspective qualitative analysis. *Journal of Child Psychology and Psychiatry, 64*(2), 265–276.
2 Greenspan, S. B., Carr, S., Woodman, A. C., Cannava, A., & Li, Y. (2022). Identified protective factors to support psychological well-being among gender diverse autistic youth. *Journal of LGBT Youth*, 1–34. https://doi.org/10.1080/19361653.2022.2119188
3 Harner, V., & Johnson, I. M. (2021). At the intersection of trans and disabled. In *Social work and health care practice with transgender and nonbinary individuals and communities*; S. K. Kattari, M. Killian Kinney, L. Kattari, and N. Eugene Walls (Eds.), Taylor & Francis.

4 Van der Loos, M. A., Hannema, S. E., Klink, D. T., Den Heijer, M., & Wiepjes, C. M. (2022). Continuation of gender-affirming hormones in transgender people starting puberty suppression in adolescence: A cohort study in The Netherlands. *The Lancet Child & Adolescent Health*. https://doi.org/10.1016/s2352-4642(22)00254-1

5 *TPS stands opposed to legislation undermining gender affirming care*. (2021). Texas Pediatric Society | The Texas Chapter of the American Academy of Pediatrics. https://txpeds.org/tps-stands-opposed-legislation-undermining-gender-affirming-care

6 *Gender-Affirming Therapy*. (2021). Psychiatry.org. https://www.psychiatry.org/psychiatrists/cultural-competency/education/transgender-and-gender-nonconforming-patients/gender-affirming-therapy

7 *Pediatricians say state bills would harm transgender youths*. (2021, March 9). aap.org. https://publications.aap.org/aapnews/news/12780

8 *AACAP statement responding to efforts to ban evidence-based care for transgender and gender diverse*. (2019). AACAP. https://www.aacap.org/AACAP/Latest_News/AACAP_Statement_Responding_to_Efforts-to-ban_Evidence-Based_Care_for_Transgender_and_Gender_Diverse.aspx

9 Adelson, S. L., & the American Academy of Child and Adolescent Psychiatry (AACAP) Committee on Quality Issues (CQI). (2012). Practice parameter on gay, lesbian, or bisexual sexual orientation, gender non-conformity, and gender discordance in children and adolescents. *Journal of the American Academy of Child & Adolescent Psychiatry*, *51*, 957–974. http://dx.doi.org/10.1016/j.jaac.2012.07.004

10 American Academy of Child and Adolescent Psychiatry (AACAP) Sexual Orientation and Gender Identity Issues Committee. (2018). *Conversion therapy policy statement*. https://www.aacap.org/AACAP/Policy_Statements/2018/Conversion_Therapy.aspx

11 Olson, K. R., Durwood, L., DeMeules, M., & McLaughlin, K. A. (2016). Mental health of transgender children who are supported in their identities. *Pediatrics*, *137*(3), e20153223.

12 Ryan, C., Russell, S. T., Huebner, D., Diaz, R., & Sanchez, J. (2010). Family acceptance in adolescence and the health of LGBT young adults. *Journal of Child and Adolescent Psychiatric Nursing*, *23*(4), 205–213.

13 Substance Abuse and Mental Health Services Administration. (2014). *A practitioner's resource guide: Helping families to support their LGBT children*. HHS Publication No. PEP14-LGBTKIDS. Rockville, MD: Substance Abuse and Mental Health Services Administration. https://store.samhsa.gov/system/files/pep14-lgbtkids.pdf

14 *2022 National survey on LGBTQ youth mental health*. (2022). thetrevorproject.org. https://www.thetrevorproject.org/survey-2022/#anti-transgender-legislation

15 Downing, J., Holt, S. K., Cunetta, M., Gore, J. L., & Dy, G. W. (2022). Spending and out-of-pocket costs for genital gender-affirming surgery in the US. *JAMA Surgery*, *157*(9), 799. https://doi.org/10.1001/jamasurg.2022.2606

16 *Press release | Press office | SSA*. (October 19, 2022). The United States Social Security Administration. https://www.ssa.gov/news/press/releases/2022/#10-2022-3

17 Office of Public and Intergovernmental Affairs. (January 12, 2022). VA.gov | Veterans affairs. VA.gov Veterans Affairs. https://www.va.gov/opa/pressrel/pressrelease.cfm?id=5753

18 *2022 national survey on LGBTQ youth mental health*. (2022). thetrevorproject.org. https://www.thetrevorproject.org/survey-2022/#anti-transgender-legislation

19 *The wage gap among LGBTQ+ workers in the United States*. (2019). Human Rights Campaign. https://www.hrc.org/resources/the-wage-gap-among-lgbtq-workers-in-the-united-states

Chapter 10

Medical Experiences

Although this book will not explore the specifics of each medical field (go to the back of the book for some recommended resources for this), there are a few over-arching experiences that occur so often that they must be acknowledged here.

Using an Assessment Scale

Use of a pain scale has been long implemented in almost all medical fields. (This is when a medical provider asks the patient, "on a scale of 1–10, how bad does the problem area hurt?") However, this does not provide a full picture. In addition to the use of the pain scale, it is recommended that the provider also uses a distress scale. (For example, "on a scale of 1–10, how distressing is this problem for you?") This allows for the capturing of the person's baseline experience. For example, a person's pain may be at a 9, but if this is common for them due to a chronic medical condition, it may not be distressing. This could account for why the patient may be simultaneously in excruciating pain but not panicking. Alternatively, a typically pain-free patient may have a 4 level on the pain scale but a 9 on the distress scale, which would indicate a possible need for mental health support or the need to con-sider including anti-anxiety medication during treatment.

Medical Gaslighting

This occurs when a patient is told that the problems or symptoms that they are reporting are imaginary, exaggerated, or being invented for attention. As a result, the patient's medical needs remain unmet and they are taught not to trust their body, their experience, or medical professionals. Over time, this can result in treatable conditions becoming much more severe, critical, or terminal due to delayed treatment and the patient can experience significant fears, phobias, or even

DOI: 10.4324/9781003167303-11 **47**

post-traumatic stress disorder (PTSD) or complex post-traumatic stress disorder (CPTSD) due to their prior experiences with medical providers. While this can happen to anyone, it is most likely to occur within systemically harmed communities including the LGBT+ community. Patients who are in multiple under-respected and under-studied communities are at greater risk of this occurring. As such, entire communities may be less likely to seek care or trust providers, especially those not within their own community. This can become generational within families of origin and within chosen families. This must be considered and may require a lengthier appointment, more outreach into those communities, and more compassion for fears related to disclosure of symptoms, acceptance of medications or treatments, and continuity of care.

Trans Broken Arm Syndrome

Even in the most inclusive cities, many transgender people continue to experience Trans Broken Arm Syndrome. In a paper for the *Journal of Research on Women and Gender* in 2016 called "'Trans broken arm': Health care stories from transgender people in rural areas,"[1] this often-experienced situation is one in which a transgender person may seek medical care for their broken arm, but the medical providers will only notice and focus on them being transgender. Though the person's genitalia has nothing to do with their injury, this is all that the providers focus on, thus leaving the person in continued pain and without resolution to their problem, while also having to defend their identity which is not a problem.

Sex Education

While this topic is often seen as controversial, this is not going to be a debate or discussion about who should teach whom about which aspects of sexuality and gender. In your role as a medical provider, this may never come up (if you work in billing, Human Resources, or the janitorial departments, for example). For others, direct patient care may mean answering questions about these topics. This may range from answering a patient's questions about their own experience, helping them to talk with someone in their lives, or working with a local school to provide insights. While your professional Code of Ethics likely discusses providing accurate information based on research and scientific best practices, it may not offer you guidance on more details. You may need to refer to handbooks specific to the school or facility where you are being asked if you need support in what you are permitted to say, depending on where you live and work.

It is also critical to consider the impact of race when thinking about inclusive and accurate sexual education. According to a 2019 report by the Black Girls Equity Alliance, "out of the 25 states with the largest Black population, only

11 mandate sex education and only three of those 11 require that the information taught is medically accurate. Hall attributed the lack of sex education, in part, to the ways sex and sexuality are spoken about in a negative way—especially in the Black church, which she grew up in."[2]

HIV and AIDS

Although it is often assumed that AIDS is a diagnosis of the past, this is inaccurate. It is only a nonproblem in communities in which there is access to diagnostic tools and treatment. As a result, some in poorer communities may not receive their diagnosis until the virus has become AIDS. In addition, some immigrants may not have access to diagnostic tools. Even in communities where early diagnosis and treatment occurs, it cannot be assumed that AIDS is not impacting the patient or the community. For many, the memories and losses of AIDS in the 1980s–1990s are still quite hard. Some lost the loves of their lives while others entered the dating world at a time when their elders were experiencing these losses, teaching them not to attempt romantic relationships. For others, the public judgment of those who experienced stigma due to AIDS led them to remain in the closet for longer or indefinitely. Older family members whose understanding of LGBT+ people is only tied to the AIDS epidemic may be perpetuating stereotypes and hateful language, causing harm within the family and within the community. You may even hear some of these assumptions expressed within your facility.

As medications to manage HIV are ever-expanding and evolving, it is critical that care providers maintain an ongoing education of statistics, treatments, and experiences. This can then be shared with patients. Topics may include the way that undetectable now equals untransmittable (U=U) which allows HIV+ and HIV− people to engage in safe sex, new access to medications, public insurance changing their coverage of different medications, and changes to who the higher demographics are for new infections.

Menstruation/Periods

Many children learn about menstruation in a binary-gendered way. Schools that teach anything often divide the students by gender assigned at birth, having the girls learn about their periods while the boys spend time roughhousing in the gym. As a result, girls are taught that this is shameful and a secret while boys have no idea about this topic at all. Plus, transgender, gender variant, and intersex children often remain clueless too or, worse, they are reminded that their body and societal expectations of their experiences do not match.

When discussing these topics with children or parents, it is important to use nongendered language. "People who menstruate" rather than "women" allow for the speaker to specifically speak about those whose bodies have this experience. This is not only about transgender people but also recognizing that not all people assigned female at birth menstruate. (Some who do not menstruate include some people with an eating disorder, some Little People, some with specific birth control regimens, those who have had a hysterectomy, some who are pregnant, and many others.) The experience of menstruation can also be a difficult time for many, as there is so much gender tied in. Many packages of pads, tampons, cups, and other supplies are found in a grocery aisle called "feminine hygiene products," which ascribes gender and causes some to feel judged for how they choose to handle their bodies because only specific ways are considered "hygienic." Much of the packaging itself as well as the commercials have a young thin blonde able-bodied person on it and/or come in pink wrapping, often with flowery scents. For anyone who does not look like the packaging, who does not identify with items wrapped in pink, or who does not want to smell like perfume, each purchase and use of these products can be a many times daily reminder of not fitting into someone's expectations. For those whose gender identity does not align with their body, the need to regularly change tampons, pads, empty cups, etc. is an ongoing reminder that their body is not aligned with their identity. As a result, many may struggle with their mental health as their period approaches and/or during their periods.

There are many free resources online that offer guidance and visual aids to discuss these topics in an inclusive way. Just remember to seek them out and to be intentional and inclusive in your daily language surrounding these topics.

Endometriosis and Adenomyosis

Although there are far too many conditions to discuss within this book (see the resource guide and other brilliant books and talks by medical specialists for more on a specific diagnosis or procedure as you may need), when discussing these medical topics, the author feels it is vital to recognize and remember that we can harm people by using gendered language. For example, although endometriosis and adenomyosis impact millions worldwide, they are often talked about as women's health issues. This is because some estimates say 10%–20% of people with a uterus experience at least one of these tough-to-diagnose conditions and many of us assume that everyone with a uterus is a woman. Unfortunately, the language around this can lead anyone assigned female at birth to be left out of both the conversation and the screening questions. (As a reminder, transgender men, some nonbinary people, some gender fluid people, and some agender people may have uteruses.) Screenings for these diseases are critical for health, fertility, and as potential causes of pain and other medical complications. Although already far too often misdiagnosed or assumed to be women exaggerating their period pain, tens of thousands suffer daily because they are ignored or medically gaslit by providers who do not recognize the symptoms as being signs of endometriosis and/or adenomyosis.

As each of these diagnoses can lead to excruciating pain, bowel and bladder issues, menstruation and pregnancy issues, and more, they (like many other diagnoses) are critical to consider for all patients and are far too often not ruled in or out for those who do not fit the thin, cisgender, heterosexual, and able-bodied expectation that some hold. While moving through this book, it is recommended that each reader think about their own area of specialty and reconsider whether the information they use to assess and diagnose patients is inclusive of all genders, all sexualities, all bodies, and all identities. Remember too to consider race, ethnicity, and other identifiers. It is often white middle-class people used in clinical studies so those who identify as anything else may not be screened properly if their symptoms do not fit the taught criteria. As a result, some groups of people suffer needlessly.

> Again, there are books and other resources written about this, with trainings online and social media accounts dedicated to these topics in more specialized areas. This book is intended for a more introductory and overarching approach, so please seek out those resources specific to your professional area of practice.

Pregnancy

Pregnancy is often a time in which gender assumptions occur. We often see clothing as "maternity-wear" and language such as "mother to be." As a result, those who are transgender, agender, or nonbinary can feel left out of their own pregnancy experience. Mindfulness around assumptions that the pregnant person is a woman and becoming a mother as well as that the baby will have a mother and father are critical in being inclusive of all people. This not only harms gender diverse people but also those in same-gender relationships and those who are becoming parents without partners whether by choice or due to circumstance. Language like "parental leave" rather than "maternity leave" and "chestfeeding" instead of "breastfeeding" can help ensure that all people are able to be their authentic selves while experiencing pregnancy and becoming a parent.

Often, small talk is made when a person is pregnant which involves asking if the person knows if they are "having a boy or a girl." Sometimes questions are asked about gender reveal parties. Although it is possible to know whether the fetus has external or internal genitalia, we know that gender is not known until the child is able to speak and self-identifies. In other words, we perpetuate incorrect information when asking about gender since this cannot be known for years after birth. We also perpetuate incorrect wording when we refer to a sex reveal party as a gender reveal party, as these events only acknowledge whether the fetus has a penis, not the gender identity of the person the fetus is becoming.

Pregnant While Black

It is critical that acknowledgment occurs that pregnancy is a major medical experience. The body shifts and changes in ways that can impact the person permanently as well as being life-threatening in some circumstances. In America, there is a significantly higher mortality rate for pregnant people who are Black or African-American.[3] As there are already many issues related to racial injustices within the medical experience, this book will not dive fully into this; however, it is recommended that those who have this insight or seek it out also consider the intersectionality of being Black/AA and also LGBT+. (Of course, other racial and identity disparities exist, so those who work in Asian populations, immigrant populations, and so on ought to seek out books and training specific to these identities and consider the intersection between them and LGBT+ identities.)

Trans Hormones during Pregnancy

It is also important to use inclusive language when discussing pregnancy, from the risks of becoming pregnant to those who are wanting to become pregnant. Not all girls/women have a uterus while not all people with a uterus identify as girls/women. Plus, not all sexual activities should be assumed to be the combining of genitalia that can produce a pregnancy. Too often, lesbian patients get lectured about why their intake forms say they do not use birth control all because the provider automatically assumes that the woman's sexual partners are men, that she was assigned female at birth, and that her body can become pregnant. This can force a patient to disclose their sexuality, their gender assigned at birth, and their medical experiences before they have spent enough time with the clinician to feel safe doing so, thus causing patient anxiety and harming the building of rapport.

Often, those who are considering hormone use to allow their body to better match their identity are told that the use of hormones will cause them to become sterile. First, be sure you are prepared to discuss fertility in full or that you have a referral ready if you are bringing this up to a patient. They may have questions about freezing eggs or sperm, about pausing hormones in the future to bear a child, or about the use of donors or surrogates. If this is not something you know much about, you may wish to refer them elsewhere. Unfortunately, many LGBT+ people are given incorrect information about this, causing them to make medical decisions based on inaccuracies. In addition, it is critical that you remain frequently updated on these topics as the research is evolving frequently.

For many years, transgender women have been told that they have to make a choice between parenthood and identity. This is because the use of testosterone for transgender women (assigned male at birth) forced them to choose to be sterile (using estrogen) or to go off of these life-affirming hormones in order to have useable sperm. This choice has been heartbreaking for many, causing them to either lose out on biological parenting or risk their mental health by pausing their hormones in order to be able to produce sperm. However, a new procedure called extended sperm search and microfreeze (ESSM) makes retrieving that sperm possible, including for those many years into estrogen use. Dr. Arie Berkovitz, an obstetrician and gynecologist and a male fertility expert at Assuta Hospital in Rishon LeZion, Israel, created the ESSM technique in 2017 as a treatment for men with low sperm counts. With ESSM, doctors are able to find and freeze small amounts of sperm from the ejaculate without side effects; finding such samples can otherwise be difficult in people who have undergone extended hormone therapy.[4] While this is obviously new research with many more studies to be completed before it becomes commonplace, it is indicative that we must always assume new research is occurring and that we not only stay updated so we can share the information with patients but that we always encourage our patients to seek out updated information when making major medical decisions, as some of what they may have been told in the past or from friends may no longer be accurate or may no longer be considered best practice.

Transgender men (assigned female at birth) have also experienced being forced to choose hormones or pregnancy. However, newer considerations are occurring.[5] This is because the assumption has been that testosterone use and pregnancy could not coexist. However, many are reconsidering whether this should be accepted largely based on the recognition of polycystic ovarian syndrome (PCOS).[6] Those with PCOS often have testosterone levels that generally fall between those for cisgender women and cisgender men. Though infertility is sometimes a PCOS symptom, many with PCOS do become pregnant and carry a healthy fetus to term as well as deliver a healthy baby whom they are able to chestfeed. (Note, "chestfeed" is a more inclusive term than "breastfeed," as many transgender men, nonbinary people, agender people, and others do not have breasts, either by surgery or biology.)

Ending A Pregnancy

Currently, access to abortion (medical and medicinal) varies by state, with the laws changing rapidly. Those ending pregnancies due to a desire to not be pregnant or due to medical complications during pregnancy may experience significant stigma, struggles, and trauma related to the experience of ending the pregnancy, in addition to the experience of how they became pregnant or whether they wanted to be pregnant. Those with more financial privilege and the privilege of accessing care in states where abortion access is readily available may have a significantly different experience than those without these privileges. (Of course, members of already oppressed communities are less likely to be in these positions of privilege.) It is critical to be mindful of these varying experiences whether present or in the patient's history and to be aware that not all patients have or have had access to the same forms of choice and care.

Eating Disorders

One of the ways in which some transgender and gender variant people work to adjust their body to that of their gender identity is through diet and exercise. However, some may make unhealthy choices. (Those lacking access to hormones and/or surgical options and in high-risk groups are at heightened risk.) This may include caloric restriction, purging, or the use of medications with weight loss side effects in order to lessen body fat. (This typically occurs when a person assigned female at birth is seeking to lessen breast tissue or curvy hips.) It may also include intentional weight gain through binging or the use of medication with weight gain side effects in order to increase body fat. (This typically occurs when a person assigned male at birth is seeking to increase breast tissue or curves at the hips or buttocks areas.) While there is a substantial breadth of research on treatment of eating disorders in general, it is critical that the care-providing team ensure that the cause is not rooted in gender-based changes or the treatment process may be focused incorrectly. In other cases, providing access to gender affirming hormones or surgeries may cause the disordered behaviors to end without traditional eating disorder treatment methods.

Cigarettes and Alcohol Use

While smoking and drinking are impactful to all people, there is a higher prevalence of current cigarette smoking and alcohol consumption was observed among U.S. lesbian, gay, and bisexual U.S. adults. Compared with heterosexual women (10.6%), the prevalence of not currently smoking cigarettes, moderate or no drinking, maintaining a normal body weight, performing any leisure-time physical activity, and sleeping ≥7 hours per day was lower among lesbian (5.4%) and bisexual women (6.9%). Assigned male at birth transgender adults had a lower prevalence of engaging in any two of five health-related behaviors (12.3%) than did cisgender adults (18.6%) but had a higher prevalence of engaging in any three of five health-related behaviors (47.2%) than did assigned female at birth transgender adults (28.2%).[7] As a result, it is important that these major lifestyle choices (smoking, drinking, weight, physical activity, and sleeping) are discussed consistently with LGBT+ patients even more so than may typically occur in your practice.

Blood Donation

There has been an ongoing debate about blood donation, as the AIDS epidemic changed the rules. At that time, the assumption was that only gay men could become infected with AIDS, thus the change became that no gay men could donate. In recent years, this has been amended in two ways. First, the language changed to include men who have sex with men (MSM) but who do not identify as "gay." Second, the parameters are now for MSM within the past 12 months. This means that gay men, MSM, and anyone who has had sex with them cannot donate for 12 months. Since all blood is screened for HIV, this is not a necessity but rather a relic from the AIDS epidemic time, making it prejudicial with no medical reasoning. However, those with biases without medical knowledge continue to perpetuate this and further the stigma. It is important that medical professionals continue to fight against this stereotype and fight to dismantle this outdated offensive policy.

Medical Care Based on Location

Although many in inclusive cities and states have become accustomed to finding medical care providers who are inclusive, this is not an option to everyone throughout the nation. In a 2022 study in the *Journal of Gay and Lesbian Social Services*, researchers and physicians practicing in the Appalachian regions of Pennsylvania, Virginia, and West Virginia said LGBT+ patients outside of urban centers are more likely to struggle to find medical professionals that are familiar with LGBT+ issues or identities, a potential detriment to the health of sexual and gender minorities.[8] "Research into sexual and gender minorities is growing quickly, but mainly in large urban centers," the study's lead author, Zachary Ramsey of the University of West Virginia said. "There are a lot of differences between urban and rural populations for a general population, so it stands to reason that there would be a lot of differences between urban and rural LGBT+ individuals," Ramsey said. "Without more studies of LGBT+ rural individuals specifically, these differences will not be known, and policies and rural LGBT+ Center programming can only use an urban population for guidance." Researchers in that study said one driving force could be a lack of health-care professionals in places like the South and Midwest— two largely rural regions that are becoming increasingly hostile places for gender-affirming physicians to practice.[9] A 2020 study found that only 20 states had at least one surgeon capable of providing gender-affirming genital surgery to transgender adults, and most practices were located in the Northeast or the West.[10,11]

Notes

1 Knutson, D., Koch, J. M., Arthur, T., Mitchell, T. A., & Martyr, M. A. (2016). "Trans broken arm": Health care stories from transgender people in rural areas. *Journal of Research on Women and Gender, 7*(1), 30–46.
2 Brinkman, B., Garth, J., Horowitz, K. R., Marino, S., & Nestman Lockwood, K. (2019). *Black girls and sexuality education: Access. Equity. Justice.* The Black Girls Equity Alliance. https://www.gwensgirls.org/wp-content/uploads/2019/10/BGEA-Report2_v4.pdf

3 An incredible documentary about this is "Aftershock," following the stories of the deaths of Shamony Gibson and Amber Rose Isaac and the ways in which their partners have honored their lives while exploring the systemic reasons why Black and Brown women are more than three times more likely to die during childbirth.

4 *A New Procedure Could Expand Reproductive Choices for Transgender Women.* (October 21, 2022). Yahoo. https://www.yahoo.com/news/procedure-could-expand-reproductive-choices-180837682.html

5 Rodriguez-Wallberg, K., Obedin-Maliver, J., Taylor, B., Van Mello, N., Tilleman, K., & Nahata, L. (2022). Reproductive health in transgender and gender diverse individuals: A narrative review to guide clinical care and international guidelines. *International Journal of Transgender Health*, 1–19. https://doi.org/10.1080/26895269.2022.2035883

6 Legro, R. S., Schlaff, W. D., Diamond, M. P., Coutifaris, C., Casson, P. R., Brzyski, R. G., Christman, G. M., Trussell, J. C., Krawetz, S. A., Snyder, P. J., Ohl, D., Carson, S. A., Steinkampf, M. P., Carr, B. R., McGovern, P. G., Cataldo, N. A., Gosman, G. G., Nestler, J. E., Myers, E. R., Santoro, N., Eisenberg, E., Zhang, M., & Zhang, H. (2010). Total testosterone assays in women with polycystic ovary syndrome: Precision and correlation with hirsutism. *The Journal of Clinical Endocrinology & Metabolism*, *95*(12), 5305–5313. https://doi.org/10.1210/jc.2010-1123

7 Cunningham, T. J., Xu, F., & Town, M. (2018). Prevalence of five health-related behaviors for chronic disease prevention among sexual and gender minority adults—25 US states and Guam, 2016. *MMWR: Morbidity and Mortality Weekly Report*, *67*(32), 888–893. https://doi.org/10.15585/mmwr.mm6732a4

8 Ramsey, Z. S., Davidov, D. M., Levy, C. B., & Abildso, C. G. (2022). An etic view of LGBTQ healthcare: Barriers to access according to healthcare providers and researchers. *Journal of Gay & Lesbian Social Services*, *34*(4), 502–520. https://doi.org/10.1080/10538720.2022.2042452

9 *Alabama Gov. Ivey signs bill criminalizing gender-affirming care into law.* (September 21, 2022). The Hill. https://thehill.com/changing-america/respect/equality/3262961-alabama-gov-ivey-signs-bill-criminalizing-gender-affirming-care-into-law/

10 *LGBTQ+ Americans face greater health care barriers in rural areas, study finds.* (July 25, 2022). The Hill. https://thehill.com/changing-america/respect/equality/3573269-lgbtq-americans-face-greater-health-care-barriers-in-rural-areas-study-finds/

11 Terris-Feldman, A., Chen, A., Poudrier, G., & Garcia, M. (2020). How accessible is genital gender-affirming surgery for transgender patients with commercial and public health insurance in the United States? Results of a patient-modeled search for services and a survey of providers. *Sexual Medicine*, *8*(4), 664–672. https://doi.org/10.1016/j.esxm.2020.08.005

Chapter 11

Retransitioning and Detransitioning & Going Back into the Closet

Retransitioning

Much of the pushback on the concepts and experiences of transitioning come from a belief that transitioning is or may be temporary. First, let's think about that. None of us can see or know the future. As a result, there is no way to definitively prove, in this moment, how someone will identify in a year, a decade, or a lifetime. However, if we support and affirm who someone is no matter what does or does not change about them, they benefit. If we push them and deny who they are right now based on assumptions or guesses we make about who we think they may be in the future, they suffer. Why would we ever want to make someone suffer?

There are sometimes cases of retransitioning. This is defined as being a situation in which someone transitions from their gender assigned at birth to a second-gender identity, then sometime later to a third-gender identity. Research shows that this is not a sign of a lack of self-awareness but rather of life experiences and of learning new terminology to express what they know about themselves. In a 2022 study, researchers found that "Participants described various paths to retransitions, including that some youth identified differently over time, and that some youth learned about a new identity (e.g., nonbinary) that fit them better.... No participants spontaneously expressed regret over initial transitions."[1] Why might this happen? Think of it much like a student choosing a college major. There are some who enter college at approximately age 18 with a plan in mind (it may be their own or what their loved ones are pushing them into). They begin classes. Some find that it is a fit for them. Others begin to realize this is not aligned with who they are, so they soul-search and choose a new path, changing majors. Sometimes

DOI: 10.4324/9781003167303-12

this is a better fit, as they now have more experience and access to different college courses. However, some realize that this fit is not quite right and discover the right fit for them only after spending more time exploring courses and figuring out where they align. (Many medical professionals were not pre-med on Day 1 of their undergraduate experience. It does not mean they are not now in the right career for them, it simply means that it took them some self-exploration to find the career that they were meant to have.)

Detransitioning & Going Back into the Closet

These experiences are often presented as proof that gender identity and/or nonheterosexuality are not valid or real nor should they be respected and affirmed. While research shows that 99.7% of people have no regrets about their transition, for the .3% who revert to their gender assigned at birth, this is not all it appears.[2] In most cases, this occurs because of external pressure. As previously discussed, many are ostracized from their families when they come out. They are less likely to be hired, more likely to be paid less, and are less often promoted in the workplace. There are struggles in society to be accepted and safe. These experiences can lead some to decide that their truth and their identity are not worth these losses and risks. This may lead them to decide to mitigate the harm they have experienced and try to live publicly as the gender or sexuality that is more accepted.

In these situations, the person may begin dressing in gender neutral ways, avoiding anything that would be obviously tied to any gender identity. This allows them to present as others want them to be while being as least-harmful to who they really are as possible. They may avoid formal gatherings where attire cannot be jeans/t-shirt and instead require a dress or suit, forcing a gendered experience. They may begin to go by a gender-neutral name in hopes of finding a balance of not upsetting others while not having to answer to a name that is not congruent with their true identity. They may give up the idea of romantic relationships and become celibate. They may request depression or anxiety medication, both due to the hardship, this causes them and because they hope for a lessened libido as a side effect. Some may become more introverted, preferring not to lie and to instead avoid others. Others may become more extroverted, trying to fill their time with others so they do not have to face the heartbreak of pretending to be who they are not.

Elders may seem less likely to go back into the closet since their parents have likely died and they are often no longer in the workplace. However, in an AARP survey last year, "34% of all LGBT survey respondents reported being at least somewhat worried about having to hide their identity to access suitable housing options as they age as did more than half (54%) of transgender and gender-expansive participants. The possibility of being forced to hide one's identity to receive long-term care is also a concern for just under half of lesbian, gay, and bisexual respondents and for 70% of transgender and gender-expansive respondents."[3] "Many in the LGBT+ community face significant discriminatory barriers when seeking housing in their older years, in fact, they go back into the closet to hide their identity in order to move into traditional senior housing," said Dr. Imani Woody, the president and CEO of Mary's House for Older Adults, a not-for-profit organization created to serve LGBT+ elders experiencing housing insecurity and isolation.[4,5]

Notes

1 Durwood, L., Kuvalanka, K. A., Kahn-Samuelson, S., Jordan, A. E., Rubin, J. D., Schnelzer, P., Devor, A. H., & Olson, K. R. (2022). Retransitioning: The experiences of youth who socially transition genders more than once. *International Journal of Transgender Health, 23*(4), 409–427. https://doi.org/10.1080/26895269.2022.2085224

2 Jedrzejewski BY, Marsiglio MC, Guerriero J, Penkin A, Berli JU; OHSU Transgender Health Program "Regret and Request for Reversal" workgroup. "Regret after Gender Affirming Surgery - A Multidisciplinary Approach to a Multifaceted Patient Experience". Plast Reconstr Surg. 2023 Jan 24. doi: 10.1097/PRS.0000000000010243. Epub ahead of print. PMID: 36727823.

3 Cantave, C. (2022). *Dignity 2022: The experience of LGBTQ older adults.* AARP. https://www.aarp.org/research/topics/life/info-2022/lgbtq-community-dignity-2022/

4 Hannon, K. (October 25, 2022). *Activist: Many LGBTQ retirees 'go back into the closet' to find senior housing.* Yahoo Finance—Stock Market Live, Quotes, Business & Finance News. https://finance.yahoo.com/news/aging-lgbtq-senior-housing-153202196.html

5 *A new procedure could expand reproductive choices for transgender women.* (October 21, 2022). Yahoo. https://www.yahoo.com/news/procedure-could-expand-reproductive-choices-180837682.html

Additional Useful Terminology for Section I

Microaggression

Subtle, indirect, or unintentional discrimination against someone for their identity. Often, individuals use microaggressions to let someone in a marginalized group know that they are unwanted or unwelcome while still being able to feign cluelessness if they are confronted about their behavior. In other cases, microaggressions can occur when unintended ignorance leads a provider or colleague to make a comment that is well-meaning but is inappropriate and offensive. An organization-wide refusal to ignore microaggressions or second guess a person who reports them helps to lessen their frequency. Each provider or employee who consistently works to learn about marginalized groups (such as by reading this book) helps to lessen the likelihood of accidental microaggressions.

These are often the toughest situations for LGBT+ people, as they appear small, can be easily dismissed by others, and may be intentionally set up to appear to be accidental. However, they become "death by a thousand cuts" and can not only continue to harm and undermine an employee or patient, but can also significantly impact the person's ability to be successful and to feel supported in the workplace, especially if others deny these are occurring. If someone tells you about them, be quick to support them, not to dismiss them. The more mindful you are, the more you can be another pair of eyes looking out for these and supporting those around you by validating their experiences.

Homophobia

The intense fear and hatred of or discomfort with people who love and are attracted to members of the same gender.

DOI: 10.4324/9781003167303-13

Transphobia

The intense fear and hatred of or discomfort with people whose gender identity or gender expression does not match or conform to cultural gender norms.

> So often, we think of homophobia and transphobia as being violent. However, they are also a sense of discomfort. While assaulting someone for their identity is homophobia/transphobia, so is not inviting someone to your party because you aren't sure if they'll bring a same gender date or not talking to someone specifically because you aren't sure what name to call them. If your discomfort is due to not wanting to get it wrong and upset the person, talk with them privately to gain clarity, don't avoid or ostracize them!

Internalized Homophobia or Transphobia

When self-identification of societal stereotypes results in a person hating who they are, causing them to dislike or resent their sexual orientation or gender identity.

> We do this often! Many women get breast implants because society says they should hate their small breasts, many men get hair plugs because they are told that masculinity or attractiveness is tied to hair. They hate aspects of themselves that do not fit into societal messaging. It's the same thing here!

Questions and Answers

Q: How do I know what to call someone if I think they might be LGBT+?

A: If you aren't sure what name to call someone, ask for their name, and they'll tell you. This is the same for any person whose name you forgot. This is also the same for someone who was named Carter Joel, who prefers to be called CJ. This isn't something specific to the LGBT+ community, although many feel anxious out of fear of offending a person in the LGBT+ community. In this case, when it comes to someone's name, it is just the same as anyone else's name, but you do not know, do not remember, or cannot recall what version of their name they may choose to go by.

Q: What about pronouns? How do I know whether to use he or she or...?

A: If you are uncertain about pronouns, ask, "What pronouns do you use?" It is considered most appropriate to ask the question that way, rather than to ask, "What is your preferred pronoun?" This is because "preferred" indicates that this is about preference and not about identity. You're not asking a person which version of a pronoun they might prefer, like the way you may ask me if I prefer chocolate or vanilla ice cream and I might like one more than the other. Instead, you are asking what pronoun they use, just the way that someone might ask what racial background you are or height you are; this is not what a person prefers—it is who they are. You may hear someone introduce themselves with their name, followed by the pronouns they use. For example, when a person introduces themselves and includes their pronouns, they may say, "Hi, I'm Rachel, she, her, hers." That means that their name is Rachel and they identify using female pronouns. If you were to tell someone that this person agreed to go to the store, you would say, "Rachel said she can go to the store." If you said, "Rachel said he can go to the store," that would not feel right to them, and it would not be a fit with how they identify.

Some prefer to use a pronoun that is neither male nor female. The introduction to such a person would sound like, "Hi, I'm Melvin, they, them, theirs." On many computer programs, this will be underlined as a mistake because "they" and "theirs" are known to have been plural, and you are using the pronoun for one individual person. This may require you to correct your word processing program. This is because the English language has not yet offered a singular nonbinary gender pronoun, although this is common in many other languages. However, the Merriam-Webster dictionary now accepts they/them/their as singular pronouns too.

Research Your Resources

Although the workplace may theoretically be only a place where work occurs, in reality, many workers spend more time in the office and with colleagues than in their homes with their families. As a result, it is likely that a medical provider will spend significant time getting to know those they work with, including both patients and colleagues. This may include experiences related to celebrations of marriages, births, and career advancement. It is also realistic that it may include knowing when a person is struggling or suffering in their personal life. In most medical settings, there is a general awareness among staff regarding community resources for those in need. For example, if an employee or patient becomes combative or violent, the police are called. If there is an injury beyond the purview of the facility's ability, the paramedics are called, and the person is taken to the hospital. If a patient or staff member is unexpectedly in need of a home or food, they are referred to local homeless shelters, food pantries, and donation services. Sounds familiar, right?

But what if those referrals exacerbate the problem or put the person at higher risk of injury or mistreatment?

You also want to be mindful of who is most inclusive amongst your colleagues. This way, you'll have some go-to people to connect your patient with if they self-identify to you. This helps to ensure that the patient can get their medical needs met by someone who is affirming and inclusive, without the heartbreaking horrors of experiencing discrimination amidst their vulnerable time of requiring medical care.

Safety and Medical Emergencies on Medical Grounds

As you continue through the process of becoming more aware of the needs of LGBT+ people in your medical community, take the time to research the organizations and resources that are commonly utilized (or even mandated by protocol). Find out whether the police and paramedics have been trained to treat LGBT+

DOI: 10.4324/9781003167303-15

people and, if they say they are, ask for information about what that training entails and whether it is mandated to everyone. Reach out to the local hospital or hospitals and find out about their policies and training programs for LGBT+ patients and families. Ask about specific support offered and skills training for this specific population. In addition, consider what information these professionals would request or require from the medical professional in the event of an emergency situation. Are your medical records up to date? How quickly are they changed to include gender identity or name changes, as needed? What are your medical facility's rules on how much information is provided, and what are considered protected details of a patient's or staff member's life?

Health and Wellness Concerns at Home

Over your years or decades working in medical facilities, it is likely that you will encounter many patients and employees whose families are struggling financially. This may occur for a variety of reasons that are incredibly common. It may also occur if a person in the family is LGBT+ identified, as this population is consistently underpaid and struggles to find and maintain employment in areas where discrimination against LGBT+ people remains. Regardless of what causes a family not to have enough money to cover all of their living expenses, these situations do happen. As such, you are likely to encounter situations where a family may be or become homeless and/or food insecure. They may need assistance in purchasing medical supplies and clothing. It is likely that your medical facility or organization already has a document prepared with a list of local homeless shelters, food pantries, and thrift or free stores. However, not every organization is accepting and affirming of LGBT+ people. Some use their religious affiliation as the reason they are not accepting. Others claim to have values that are based on their founder's upbringing many generations ago. Whatever the reasoning, it is not helpful to the family to refer them somewhere where they will be ridiculed and/or turned away when they are most in need of support.

Take the time to review and research the locations on the existing list. Look into the overarching organizations that fund or sponsor each program. Seek out information about how families are kept together in homeless shelters and whether this changes if the family has same-gender parents or a transgender person in their family unit. Find out whether the organizations' mission statements include religion of any sort and, if so, contact them to inquire about how staff and volunteers are trained to interact with LGBT+ people. You may find that there is little or no guidance given, allowing each worker to decide whether to welcome a family in or whether to turn them away for somehow living a life that goes against the organization's expectations or beliefs.

In some cases, medical facilities may have a volunteer or community group that gathers neighbors and community leaders to put together care packages for families who cannot afford many basic items that local community need. These can be a great way to bring folks together and provide a sense of support and care within the community. However, you may also need to inquire into the practices and protocols of these groups as well as other local or federal organizations that donate holiday toys, medical supplies, or clothing in regard to how they proceed when a person's gender identity is not aligned with their gender assigned at birth. Some may allow the family to identify the person's gender and use only that to pick out gifts, medical materials, and outfits to give. Others may utilize medical or birth records and refuse to deviate. In either situation, items that are gender-normative (all pink for girls, all blue for boys) may not be a fit for many of the adults in your medical facility, and this may be a conversation to have with the organization for overarching reasons, not just for employees who identify as a gender minority.

Safety Emergencies Occurring at Home

In addition to emergency situations within the medical facility and difficult times at home, LGBT+ people may become unsafe at home due to their sexual and/or gender identity. This may result in physical, emotional, psychological, or even sexual abuse. It may result in significant neglect of the person's basic needs. Sometimes this is rooted in a parent or guardian or spouse or partner's anger about the situation. Sometimes it is a misguided attempt to change the person into something more acceptable to the angry person. You may see physical damage or begin to see the person's their behavior change, or they may begin to struggle with making appointments or come into the office disheveled or appearing to be malnourished or unwashed. Unfortunately, not all homeless shelters or emergency centers are inclusive of LGBT+ people, so it is wise to know the options before recommending them to someone who appears to be in need.

The goal is simply to be prepared for an LGBT+ person in need so that you are ready to act at the time the need arises, rather than trying to juggle the emergent situation and completing research to ensure their safety as you transfer or refer them to the care of others.

Trans Joy

Throughout this book, much of the focus is on the problems, risks, and bigotry experienced by transgender people throughout their lives and, too often, throughout each day. While this is critical to understand how to best provide compassionate and affirming care, it can be easy for a person to become so focused on this aspect of life that they begin to see transgender people as sad or wounded or traumatized or fragile. Like all demographics, transgender people are not a monolith, as such, some may fit into each of those categories at one time or another. However, this is not all of whom any transgender person is, nor is it affirming to assume that the transgender patient/colleague/person in front of you fits into one of those categories at this very moment (or perhaps ever).

As such, we have to be mindful that much of the transgender life experience is rooted in having and/or seeking joy, just like everyone else. As you move through this book and through life, it is important to seek out not just areas in which you can advocate for transgender people's right to life, to safety, and to supportive care but also to joy.

This is also critical when considering intersectionality. This is sometimes addressed in the Black community, with recognition that, while Black Lives Matter is true and critical, it is not enough to just think that Black people's lives matter. Mattering is the bare minimum and focusing only on mattering is harmful because it sets the bar far too low for how Black people deserve to be treated. Based on this, the Black community has created often-used hashtags including #BlackGirlMagic, #BlackMenSmile, and #BlackBoyJoy. The intention is that, when the positive is shown, not only does it promote further positivity within the Black community, it also shows non-Black people that Black people are not just the horrible things that are done to them but that they are entire people with happiness, exuberance, and experiences that bring them bliss.

As you move through this book, you may be tempted to continue to surround yourself with incoming updated knowledge about what is happening within the transgender community and/or within the Black transgender/Asian transgender/Disabled transgender communities. Great! You can do this by following social media accounts of activists and community organizers. As you do this, I encourage

DOI: 10.4324/9781003167303-16

you to also choose to follow hashtags and accounts that focus on the joy of life too. This may include accounts where stories of gender euphoria are filmed, where happy coming out stories are shared, and where you can view regular lives of regular people who just so happen to also be in one or more of the LGBT+ identity categories.

In Closing

It is important to hear and understand terminology from the perspective of those you are engaging in conversation with. Using a person's chosen term without judgment can make all the difference in the world. This means being open at all times, regardless of whether you understand why a staff member or patient in your office has chosen to identify by a different name, gender, or a pronoun from those they have previously used in your office or in your medical records. The best course of action is to thank them for letting you know and then to use that name and pronoun. If other employees or providers question this, not every moment needs to be a reason to stop the meeting for a long lecture about these topics. It may simply be that you can say that this is the name this person is using and then continue on with your day. If you accept this information from the individual and behave as if it is no big deal, it is much more likely that the others will behave as if it is no big deal as well. However, be mindful of what may be being whispered when you are not present or things that might be said in the hallway before or after interacting with the person. You can always check in with a patient or employee before or after your interaction to ask if they are feeling safe and supported or to remind them that your office is a place where they will not be judged or mistreated. And remember, in addition to seeking out ways to lessen or end victimization and harm, it is critical to seek out examples of joy in each category of LGBT+ people, including the intersections of their identities, and to never forget that the goal is not just to stop the harm but also to increase the joy.

DOI: 10.4324/9781003167303-17

SCENARIOS

Test Your Knowledge

Section Summary

In this section, you will find scenarios that do happen, have happened, and are happening in medical facilities across America. For each, you will find a scenario situation, thought questions, and guidance.

How to Use This Section

This section can be utilized individually or collectively. If you are reading this on your own, read the scenario, take time to answer each question in your mind or on paper, and then turn the page to find out how your responses fit with the guidance by the expert, as if she was on-call to guide you through this. Then, you'll see suggested readings at the back of the book. This will allow you to imagine the potential results, receive guidance from the expert, and to find out what research indicates, or what peer-reviewed publications would be useful to buttress the situation if you were to present the scenario and the guidance to your medical in order to create or update policies. If you are reading this as a group, the scenario can be read aloud and the questions answered collectively; or the scenarios can be assigned to different breakout groups for consideration, discussion, and sharing with the larger group.

Section Take-Away

The purpose of this section is to imagine and examine what would happen if the provided scenario situation occurred in your own medical facility or workplace, and to become more thoughtful about the various ways of handling each situation.

DOI: 10.4324/9781003167303-18

Scenario 1

A female employee in your medical practice named Jessica has just come up to you before the start of an important all-staff and asked to speak with you privately. She discloses that she is transgender. She asks that you call her James and that you use male pronouns both privately and during the meeting. You have never had a transgender employee before and are uncertain how to proceed.

1. If you were the sole decision-maker at your medical facility, how would you choose for your medical facility to handle this situation?

2. Based on what you know of those in decision-making positions at your medical facility, what decision do you think they would make about how you must handle this situation?

3. Utilizing only your medical facility's employee handbook, what (if anything) do they dictate about how you must handle this situation?

4. If the answer to question #1 is different from the answers to question #2 and/or question #3, what can you do, in your role in the medical facility? What (if anything) should you do?

SCENARIO 1.1

In addition to the information provided in Scenario 1, the employee discloses to you that their spouse knows about them being transgender, and they are "not at all okay with this." At the moment the employee makes this statement, other employees begin entering your office for the meeting. There is no time for further conversation with the employee without others overhearing.

1. If you were the sole decision-maker at your medical facility, how would you choose for your medical facility to handle this situation?

2. Based on what you know of those in decision-making positions at your medical facility, what decision do you think they would make about how you must handle this situation?

3. Utilizing only your medical facility's employee handbook, what (if anything) do they dictate about how you must handle this situation?

4. If the answer to question #1 is different from the answers to question #2 and/ or question #3, what can you do, in your role in the medical facility? What (if anything) should you do?

GUIDANCE

First, pat yourself on the back! This employee feels safe enough to share this with you, which means you are doing a great job modeling what it looks like when someone in the workplace is trustworthy. Next, get more information from this employee. Has James told others in the workplace? Will James be telling his colleagues directly or just letting them figure it out when he is called on in meeting by a different name? How does James want you to handle each of those situations if not everyone knows? Also, ask about James' emotions and consider his safety. Does James feel safe at work and at home? Have you noticed James' work quality slipping or him appearing to be struggling with anxiety or depression?

Now that you've gathered the facts, ask if he wants you to change all of your written records to reflect what James has told you. If he is not yet ready, tell him that you await his word and will act when he gives it. When he is ready, make sure that the documents you use for all Human Resources forms, for all name tags and security badges, etc., all say "James." This helps to ensure that James is called on appropriately. If you utilize computers or if anything is hung up in your office with employee names, change the name to James. This will allow James to continue to be in the office as himself, without having to log into a computer program using the name he does not use or seeing items on the wall with a name that is no longer his name.

When considering Scenario 1.1, this requires more information. Ask to see this employee after the meeting and ask if this means that he does not feel safe at home. If there is threat or experience of physical or emotional violence, proceed following the medical facility's mandated protocol for staff member abuse. If you live in an area that is very anti-LGBT+ or promotes conversion camps, offer James the number of a suicide prevention hotline such as The Gay, Lesbian, Bisexual and Transgender National Hotline, The Trans Lifeline, Trevor Project Lifeline or The GLBT National Youth Talkline (geared toward youth but their specific training in LGBT+ callers may still prove useful), The SAGE hotline (geared toward LGBT+ elders but also offering peer support, which may be helpful for adults of any age), or a national suicide prevention lifeline or crisis text line so he can gain support from professionals who are understanding and accepting of his identity. Continue to check in regularly with James.

Scenario 2

It is time for a large quarterly company meeting in which many teams come together. You spot Mr. Johnson, one of the medical facility's eldest and most beloved leaders. As you begin to approach him to say hello, you notice he is wearing pants, a blouse, and heels. When he turns around to greet you, you notice he is wearing lipstick. He notices your surprise and tells you that, since the last quarterly meeting, he came out to his family, and now he is "finally getting to be called Mrs. Johnson." You are unsure whether the company leadership or other staff members know about this.

1. If you were the sole decision-maker at your medical facility, how would you choose for your medical facility to handle this situation?

2. Based on what you know of those in decision-making positions at your medical facility, what decision do you think they would make about how you must handle this situation?

3. Utilizing only your medical facility's employee handbook, what (if anything) do they dictate about how you must handle this situation?

4. If the answer to question #1 is different from the answers to question #2 and/or question #3, what can you do, in your role in the medical facility? What (if anything) should you do?

GUIDANCE

There are three things happening simultaneously here: your surprise, their happiness about their open identity as Mrs. Johnson, and you're wondering if others know about this. Let's start with that last one. Since you're coming into a meeting for all staff, whether others already know about this or are about to be surprised by this doesn't much matter, because soon the room will fill up and everyone will know. Since the lipstick and the introduction as Mrs. Johnson clued you in, they will likely do the same as others enter the room. So, there's no need to wonder, worry, or concern yourself with what others know. You don't even need to worry about you knowing what others do not, as Mrs. Johnson is not only choosing to wear a shade of lipstick that is obvious, but she is also openly talking about herself as Mrs. Johnson—and she is making a point of saying how happy she is about being Mrs. Johnson.

This just leaves your surprise and Mrs. Johnson's happiness about openly being Mrs. Johnson. While your surprise will dissipate as the new information becomes information you've known for longer and longer, what stands is Mrs. Johnson's happiness about openly being Mrs. Johnson. You can also presume that this new information may cause some comments and conversations from your peers. Mrs. Johnson isn't a fool; it is certain she knows this will probably happen, and she has likely spent days, weeks, months, or even years preparing herself for them. However, you do not need to leave her to brave that on her own. How supportive do you want to be right now?

You have three options. In order of least brave to most brave: stand or sit in the room in silence while the others in the room discuss this new information; stand or sit next to Mrs. Johnson and offer comments of support, knowing she is overhearing whatever may be being said about her; or roam the room, listening for others to talk about this and jumping in to either share words of support for Mrs. Johnson or shut down negative commentary.

While the bravest option may be tied to your seniority at the meeting or your knowledge and relationships with your peers, it also offers you the strongest opportunity to advocate and support someone who is in a vulnerable position in the room. Plus, since Mrs. Johnson has significant seniority, you would be buttressing on that while supporting her; if that does not feel like something that you can do, for whatever reason, sitting with Mrs. Johnson both to offer her words of support and to visually show solidarity can send a strong message to your peers about your beliefs concerning inclusion in medical facilities.

Let's say, though, that, at the moment, you weren't sure what to do so you just sat down for the meeting, saying nothing, and doing nothing regarding Mrs. Johnson. Now you're reading this, rethinking that moment, and wishing you would have done things differently. Whether that meeting was yesterday, last medical facility year, or a decade ago, reach out to Mrs. Johnson now! Apologize to her for missing the opportunity to support her more directly. Ask her what you can do for her now to support her. If she has already retired, take time to think about and create a plan for the next Mrs. Johnson (whether this would be a staff member or an employee). Decide how you will show your support when that person comes out to the medical facility as transgender. Then, when the moment happens, follow through. (You might even consider sending a letter to Mrs. Johnson to tell her how knowing her inspired you to act differently in the next situation.)

Scenario 3

On Friday after typical working hours, the federal government signed a bill into law that discriminates against LGBT+ people. You know that there are staff and patients at your medical facility who openly identify as LGBT+ and that there are staff and patients who have LGBT+ loved ones. It is Monday morning and you are commuting to work. You know that the new law will be brought up by both patients and colleagues, as it is considered to be major news.

Questions

1. If you were the sole decision maker at your medical facility, how would you choose for your medical facility to handle this situation?

2. Based on what you know of those in decision-making positions at your medical facility, what decision do you think they would make about how you must handle this situation?

3. Utilizing only your medical facility's student handbook and staff handbook, what (if anything) do they dictate about how you must handle this situation?

4. What can you do, in your role in the medical facility, if the answer to question #1 is different from the answers to question #2 and/or question #3? What (if anything) should you do?

SCENARIO 3.1

How might this be different if the decision was made by your state's government?

SCENARIO 3.2

How might this be different if the decision was made by your local community's government?

GUIDANCE

This is a great opportunity for conversations about the way laws get made. Give others space to share their frustrations and to talk about how they may feel helpless. Ask them to brainstorm ideas about how to let current politicians know how they feel about this decision and how they can influence the adults in their lives who can vote.

For Scenario 3.1, continue the conversation but also offer the opportunity for interested parties to find out about state-wide opportunities to speak with the politicians in your state. Encourage them to research the politicians making state-wide decisions and to find out how to be in contact with them to discuss their beliefs and how they want to encourage these state representatives to vote. This may include attending age or issue-based lobby days, it may focus on attending town hall meetings when the politician is in their area, or it may be an opportunity for the students to come together to work on requesting a visit by one or more politicians. Guiding them to do the research and to do the work not only helps them toward their goal, it encourages their activism and their sense of community as they work together to find ways to reach out to their own representatives.

Scenario 3.2 can also be responded to in this way, though the local aspect may offer even more opportunity for medical providers to speak up about their concerns and their emotions. Some may have personal ties to one or more decision-makers. It may become easier to encourage one of the decision-makers to visit the medical facility to speak with staff. It may be impactful for those who are interested to individually or collectively write a letter to be published in the local newspaper. Television news may be interested in a story talking with providers as they speak out, though encourage them to talk with the media department first. As individuals explore avenues to publicize their opinion, be sure to remind them that, as representatives of the medical practice or group, they may require permission in order to be publicizing their name or their faces.

In addition, no matter which scenario is most accurate for the situation, be sure to offer opportunities to remain aware of situations before votes or changes occur so they can work to encourage what they believe or prevent voting from occurring, rather than to always be in a reactive role. This can be done in unison as a medical facility via e-mail listservs or by sharing news story links in a group chat or on a staff bulletin board in the break room. Talking with your colleagues may guide you in how to proceed.

Scenario 4

On your way out of medical facility yesterday, you walked past an intern, Jamie, who was holding hands with another intern of the same gender. This surprised you but you said nothing. This morning, the intern approached you. Jamie says, "So I know you saw me yesterday holding hands with Mickey. Please please don't tell anyone. They'd probably judge me if they found out I'm bi." Just as the intern finishes this sentence, another staff member approaches you with a question. By the time you turn back to Jamie, they have walked away. Later that day you receive an e-mail from Jamie's attending. In the e-mail, the attending asks for your help. They say, "Jamie has been acting strange. We don't know what's going on. We thought you might have some idea."

Questions

1. If you were the sole decision maker at your medical facility, how would you choose for your medical facility to handle this situation?

2. Based on what you know of those in decision-making positions at your medical facility, what decision do you think they would make about how you must handle this situation?

3. Utilizing only your medical facility's student handbook and staff handbook, what (if anything) do they dictate about how you must handle this situation?

4. What can you do, in your role in the medical facility, if the answer to question #1 is different from the answers to question #2 and/or question #3? What (if anything) should you do?

GUIDANCE

When reading this Scenario as a whole, it can be easy to connect Jamie holding hands and identifying to you as bisexual to the e-mail from their Attending. However, that is actually unknown at this point. Before assuming a connection, it would be fair to respond to Jamie's Attending and ask for more information. This may indicate to you whether the concern is about something completely different. If the concern is clearly tied to Jamie's sexuality and their work to hide it from their peers(s), ask to speak with Jamie. Have a private conversation where Jamie can speak freely but be sure to follow medical facility's protocols. Explain to Jamie that you received an e-mail from their concerned Attending and ask for more information about whether home and work are safe for Jamie.

If there is a safety concern, follow medical facility protocol to report this. If the safety concern is unknown because Jamie is assuming home will become unsafe if Jamie comes out as bisexual, offer to help Jamie, and follow medical facility protocols for this, if they exist. If they do not, talk with decision-makers about being on the team to create a protocol so that the written rule can be as inclusive as possible. In the meantime, let Jamie know that you are working to support them and that, as such, you'd like to discuss this with the medical facility social worker and/or Human Resources. Let Jamie know that, for safety reasons, you cannot simply do nothing, so your goal is to work together to find a solution. Be sure you are documenting everything as this conversation is occurring. If you decide to seek out external resources to guide you such as The Trevor Project's hotline or a local LGBT+ organization, maintain medical facility privacy protocols at all times. Work together within the parameters of your role and bring in those with more experience in home life trauma and mental healthcare to encourage and support Jamie through offering honesty to their parent(s) while also having a safety plan in case home becomes unsafe or in case Jamie's fear of coming out causes them to behave in a way that is not safe.

Scenario 5

As part of your local school's mandated curriculum, health class is included in every student's schedule. This includes information about physical anatomy, sexual behaviors, and sexually transmitted infections, using age-appropriate language. You discover that the book used for class and the lesson plans provided by the book publisher only include cisgender bodies and heterosexual relationships. While you do not know the sexual orientations and gender identities of every student and staff member, you know that there are LGBT+ parents whose children attend the school.

Questions

1. If you were the sole decision maker at your medical facility, how would you choose for your medical facility to handle this situation?

2. Based on what you know of those in decision-making positions at your medical facility, what decision do you think they would make about how you must handle this situation?

3. Utilizing only your medical facility's handbook, what (if anything) do they dictate about how you must handle this situation?

4. What can you do, in your role in the medical facility, if the answer to question #1 is different from the answers to question #2 and/or question #3? What (if anything) should you do?

SCENARIO 5.1

Would your answers to the questions change if the class was being taught in elementary school If so, how? If not, why not?

SCENARIO 5.2

Would your answers to the questions change if the class was being taught in middle school? If so, how? If not, why not?

SCENARIO 5.3

Would your answers to the questions change if the class was being taught in high school? If so, how? If not, why not?

SCENARIO 5.4

Would your answers to the questions change if the class was being taught to high school seniors, all of whom would be 18 years old or turning 18 years old during the course term? If so, how? If not, why not?

GUIDANCE

This Scenario may seem, on its surface, as a no-win situation. It's easy to picture everyone wanting something different and you and your school being stuck in the middle, right? It doesn't have to be that way! First, look at the existing curriculum and book(s) used. Is it possible to make small additions to the materials to become more inclusive? For example, is it possible to turn a quiz about safe sex behaviors into one without genders being used, swapping out "your partner" for gendered words? Is it possible to create a statement or additional handout to provide to students to articulate why gender and sexuality are being taught and to guide them toward recognizing inclusion and lack thereof as they read? This is likely the least disruptive method of correcting the problem.

However, this may not be enough, either based on what the book information gives or because you now know enough about LGBT+ people that you want to ensure that your students receive a more well-rounded education in this class. In this case, look at the answers to your questions for this Scenario and use them to guide you through making these changes happen.

For Scenarios 5.1, 5.2, and 5.3, the biggest difference is the simplicity of the language being used and finding out whether your state or school district has requirements regarding parental notification before teaching specific materials. This will offer guidance in choosing words that are inclusive and at the level of your learners. A great example here would be to use Jazz Jennings' materials. At the elementary school level, there is a book called *I Am Jazz*. The book discusses Jazz being a transgender girl who was born with a "girl brain and a boy body." At the middle school level, she has an autobiographical book that would add to a student's understanding of the experience of a transgender teen called "Being Jazz: My Life as a (Transgender) Teen." At the high school level, it would be age appropriate for students to watch episodes or the entirety of her television series, *I Am Jazz,* which chronicles Jazz's high school years and her move through graduation and into college. Not only could any of these be used individually, a school district could decide to work together to utilize all of these platforms and effectively let their students grow up with Jazz and her story. This offers a perspective of the transgender identity through the lens of a person their own age, using life experiences and developmental milestones that are age appropriate both to Jazz and to the students engaging in Jazz's story.

As for Scenario 5.4, there may be no difference between this scenario and 5.1–5.3, depending on your school district policies. In some schools, permission slips for parental approval are no longer necessary once a student is 18 years old. If this is applicable in your school, you may be able to offer a class to students 18+ years old in which information can be shared that students would be interested to learn but that may not easily pass parental approval. This may be worth considering if your students would be interested and if you would be willing to teach it. If so, you can talk with your administrators about how to create and gain class approval so it can be offered in an upcoming school term.

Scenario 6

You are in your current role within your current medical facility. One of your employees is openly gay. Recently, you assigned a collaborative project, which is due in one week. The next day, you receive an e-mail from one of the employees, Chris. "I am writing because of the collaboration you assigned. I would like to be put in another group. In our household, we do not condone homosexuality. As such, I do not want to work in this group with the homosexual employee. In addition, please ensure that I am never assigned to group or pairs work with this employee."

1. If you were the sole decision-maker at your medical facility, how would you choose for your medical facility to handle this situation?

2. Based on what you know of those in decision-making positions at your medical facility, what decision do you think they would make about how you must handle this situation?

3. Utilizing only your medical facility's employee handbook, what (if anything) do they dictate about how you must handle this situation?

4. If the answer to question #1 is different from the answers to question #2 and/or question #3, what can you do, in your role in the medical facility? What (if anything) should you do?

SCENARIO 6.1

Would your answers to the questions be different if, instead of being openly gay, the employee was openly transgender? If so, how? If not, why not?

GUIDANCE

Depending on where you are, you may have already received an e-mail like this, or you may not be able to imagine anyone receiving an e-mail like this; American experiences vary so wildly depending on geographical locations and industries! However, since people relocate all the time, no matter how open your employee population typically is, a new employee in your workplace may come from a place where sending this type of e-mail to you seems logical and right for their beliefs. When we remove all of the details, we come down to two options here: either reassign Chris to a different group and never put Chris and the gay employee together, or refuse to condone Chris' request and treat Chris, the gay employee, and all employees the same.

As a reader of this book, you've long figured out that the goal here is typically to enforce inclusion wherever possible and to remove stigma and ignorance. Chris would very likely benefit from interacting with many different types of people, as all employees do. We would also need to know whether the medical facility policies, city policies, or state laws have mandates against discrimination against sexual orientation. If so, it would make sense to pull Chris aside and discuss the situation. First, hear Chris's thoughts and feelings on the subject. Listen to Chris' concerns, talk with Chris about the nonbullying policies that exist, let Chris know that his working with the gay employee is going to happen both now and likely on a periodic basis throughout his time with the company, and regularly check in with the group members individually and collectively to ensure a safe experience for everyone. This may also require you to include your supervisor, as sending a response to Chris' refusing to remove him from the group may create further tension or reaction by him. Your medical facility may even wish to involve legal counsel simply to protect themselves.

In other medical facilities, it is preferred to avoid conflict thus moving Chris would be facility protocol. Even then, it would be a great idea to speak with Chris. You'll also want to be sure not to cause the group members to take on additional work because of this, as it would not be right for an entire group to suffer due to Chris. For Scenario 6.1, the guidance would not change unless the medical facility's policy specifically considers gender identity the same as gender for nondiscrimination purposes. In this case, follow the same protocols as above, letting Chris know that you would not be legally permitted to make the requested changes.

Scenario 7

While walking from the cafeteria to your office, you overhear two colleagues calling a third colleague name. As you approach, you hear that the names are based on the colleague's sexual orientation. Before you get close enough to say something, the three colleagues see you and all run off in the other direction. Later, you see the third colleague alone in the hall. You ask if everything is okay. They respond, "I know you saw the whole thing earlier, but it's nothing. I mean, it's not nothing nothing, but it's no big deal. Just don't say anything, okay? Because if you say something, they'll think I said something and then it'll be way worse."

Questions

1. If you were the sole decision maker at your medical facility, how would you choose for your medical facility to handle this situation?

2. Based on what you know of those in decision-making positions at your medical facility, what decision do you think they would make about how you must handle this situation?

3. Utilizing only your medical facility's handbook, what (if anything) do they dictate about how you must handle this situation?

4. What can you do, in your role in the medical facility, if the answer to question #1 is different from the answers to question #2 and/or question #3? What (if anything) should you do?

SCENARIO 7.1

Would your answers to the questions be different if, instead of the comments being about the colleague's sexual orientation they were about the colleague's gender identity? If so, how? If not, why not?

SCENARIO 7.2

Would your answers to the questions be different depending on the professional level of the colleague? If so, how or when would the answer change? If not, why not?

GUIDANCE

For every Scenario in this section, this is based on your state's and your facility's bullying policies as well as on any local, state, and federal laws that may protect against discrimination on the basis of sexual orientation and/or gender identity (or on gender in general). Although it is very common for victims of bullying to fear upsetting the bullies, you can point out to the colleague that you witnessed the situation firsthand and that this will be stated to the bullies, to help make it clear how you became aware of the situation. In addition, while following the protocol for handling bullying situations, it may be a good idea to include Human Resources to ensure that the person being bullied can be assessed for safety and offered resources.

The only situation in which professional level may matter is if the bullying becomes a legal concern. If the actions of a bully are at or nearing legal concerns, it may be wise to include the local police or community officer in order to enlighten the individual about the legal options to press charges for harassment so that they have access to all information while making future choices.

Scenario 8

While walking down the hall, you realize that every poster promoting family support and togetherness depicts white families with a mother and a father. You know that there are members of the community in same sex marriages and students in the school who are multiracial.

Questions

1. If you were the sole decision maker at your medical facility, how would you choose for your medical facility to handle this situation?

2. Based on what you know of those in decision-making positions at your medical facility, what decision do you think they would make about how you must handle this situation?

3. Utilizing only your medical facility's handbook, what (if anything) do they dictate about how you must handle this situation?

4. What can you do, in your role in the medical facility, if the answer to question #1 is different from the answers to question #2 and/or question #3? What (if anything) should you do?

5. If asked for feedback, what is an example of what you might say and who is the best person to have this conversation with?

GUIDANCE

First, yay for you for noticing something that has likely been going on all around you for years or even decades! You noticing this indicates a growth mindset that shows you are open to learning new ideas and that you are seeking ways to include all families and people in your school. We don't know if there is a budget to purchase additional posters to add to the halls. If so, talking with the person who makes these purchases can be a great option to solve this problem.

What if there is not time to get new posters? How about involving extracurricular groups or a local school? A quick gathering of posterboard and/or using the school computers can lead students to create inclusive wall hangings quickly and it lets them own the experience of thinking about how to make the space more inclusive to everyone who may come into their school. You can assign students to support specific minority groups/types of families as you see a need, or you can task them with thinking about what types of people are not being honored or acknowledged on the walls and to create their own ideas from there. (Be sure to have them create a rough draft on scratch paper before using supplies to create the final posters so that you can ensure accurate/appropriate wording and inclusion!)

Scenario 9

After being at your medical facility for a number of years, you have become known for advising a number of activities and groups. One day during lunch, a handful of colleagues approaches, asking if you would guide them in an Employee Resource Group (ERG) they want to start. They tell you it requires no effort on your part, the group will meet weekly during lunch in your office, they just need to write your name down on the application form for approval and get you to sign it. You check your calendar and tell them that you can host their new group every Thursday. When they hand you the form for your signature, you find out that the group is an LGBT+ ERG.

Questions

1. If you were the sole decision maker at your medical facility, how would you choose for your medical facility to handle this situation?

2. Based on what you know of those in decision-making positions at your medical facility, what decision do you think they would make about how you must handle this situation?

3. Utilizing only your medical facility's handbook, what (if anything) do they dictate about how you must handle this situation?

4. What can you do, in your role in the medical facility, if the answer to question #1 is different from the answers to question #2 and/or question #3? What (if anything) should you do?

GUIDANCE

Depending on your medical facility, this may not even require any guidance! In many medical facilities, these organizations have existed for many years without incident or concern. If your facility is open to this group—and since you have read this book—you are a great fit for this and it sounds like your colleagues are excited to lead the creation and ongoing meetings, so just continue to support them the way you do all of the other groups you've advised!

If your medical facility refuses the application to begin the group, work with the medical facility to find out their reasoning. You can also offer the medical facility information about other facilities in the news who refused to allow this type of group and the ways in which it became problematic to refuse to allow all groups to gather if they meet the medical facility's group ERG creation requirements.

Scenario 10

You are a leader who is well liked in your medical facility. As such, you often hear gossip about employees in the medical facility from the employees you most frequently interact with. You have just heard that one of your employees is gay. This employee participates in your office's department-wide sports team. This means that this employee will be changing out of scrubs and into other attire in the locker room with other employees of the same gender. You are not certain whether the employee's sexuality is widely known throughout the medical facility. You are unsure how other employees feel about changing clothes in the locker room with someone who is attracted to the same gender.

1. If you were the sole decision-maker at your medical facility, how would you choose for your medical facility to handle this situation?

2. Based on what you know of those in decision-making positions at your medical facility, what decision do you think they would make about how you must handle this situation?

3. Utilizing only your medical facility's employee handbook, what (if anything) do they dictate about how you must handle this situation?

4. If the answer to question #1 is different from the answers to question #2 and/ or question #3, what can you do, in your role in the medical facility? What (if anything) should you do?

GUIDANCE

There are a lot of details in this scenario, so let's break this down into what we know for sure, removing all of the things that may be rumors, misunderstandings, or inaccuracies. When we pare this down, all we know for sure is that there are employees who think that one of your employees is gay. Before we consider anything else, the feelings of fear that others are uncomfortable with a person because they are gay indicate outdated beliefs that someone's sexuality inherently makes them less safe to be around. It also indicates that there may be a misperception that a person's being gay makes them deserve to be sexualized. It is important that you take time to consider this belief within yourself, both to change the mistaken thinking and so your inherent bias does not become foundational for employees.

In addition, when considering whether this bias may be existing for others, it is unknown whether the employee is gay, whether others are correct in their assumptions, and whether anyone cares. That is all separate from anything having to do with the locker room situation. With this in mind, your best bet is to simply check in with the employee in question. Since you do not know anything for sure about the employee's sexuality and they have not addressed it with you, a general check-in is your best approach. The intention is not to try to find out if the rumors are true or to get the employee to come out to you (if they are gay), but to ask how the employee is doing. Does the employee feel safe in the locker room? Are they being treated differently than their peers?

If, after checking in with this employee, you feel that they may be struggling, follow the medical facility's protocol for working with an employee who is struggling for any reason. This may involve including the guidance counselor, for example. Since this may be related to the employee's sexuality, talk with Human Resources.

Now that we've got a plan for the employee, let's look at the locker room situation. We don't know right now whether there are any concerns by anyone about this specific employee. However, this is a good time to check policies and procedures about how this would be handled in the event that this scenario occurred, and it was a problem. If there is a plan in place, know what it is and consider, after reading this book, whether this is the most inclusive policy. If it is, awesome! We can move on! If not, find out who to discuss this with and how to work with them to create an improved policy that is inclusive. If there is no policy at all, ask the policymaker at your medical facility if they would allow you to write that policy. If they will (or if they will allow you to write it with them), this would be a great time to create the most inclusive policy possible.

What might that look like? First, tie it into the existing anti-bullying policies. It is fairly standard that medical facility policies state that bullying is not permitted for any reason at any time anywhere on medical facility grounds or at medical facility-related events. Thus, this would include locker room bullying. Next, consider the unique nature of an LGBT+ employee. Now, think about what other groups this may be true for. This could include people with disabilities, those with anxiety, employees with trauma due to abuse, and employees who may simply not feel confident in their bodies. Suddenly, this policy stops being "just about LGBT+ employees" and now becomes a policy about many employees. (This makes it tougher for the administration to refuse.) Perhaps your locker room allows for curtains or stalls to be installed, so employees have access to private changing areas. If not (or if there are not enough), is there a nearby restroom that employees can use for added privacy?

If this is for a sports team where a uniform is required, offering options for different changing areas, staggered start times so there are fewer employees changing at a time, or having a staff member within earshot of the locker room so that any bullying would be heard and interrupted could all work well to eliminate some of the problems with locker room anxiety and stress.

Scenario 11

As part of your medical facility's mandated health insurance updated paperwork, you are provided with pamphlets given to you by the health insurance company meant to offer education to limit unhealthy practices that can lead to the need for medical treatments. You discover that the materials provided only include cisgender bodies and heterosexual relationships. While you do not know the sexual orientations and gender identities of every employee and staff member, you know that there are LGBT+ employees in the medical facility.

1. If you were the sole decision-maker at your medical facility, how would you choose for your medical facility to handle this situation?

2. Based on what you know of those in decision-making positions at your medical facility, what decision do you think they would make about how you must handle this situation?

3. Utilizing only your medical facility's employee handbook, what (if anything) do they dictate about how you must handle this situation?

4. If the answer to question #1 is different from the answers to question #2 and/or question #3, what can you do, in your role in the medical facility? What (if anything) should you do?

GUIDANCE

This scenario may seem, on its surface, as a no-win situation. It's easy to picture everyone wanting something different, and you and your medical facility are stuck in the middle, right? It doesn't have to be that way! First, look at the existing materials used. Is it possible to request that the insurance company makes small additions to the materials to become more inclusive? For example, is it possible to turn a quiz about safe-sex behaviors into one without genders being used, swapping out "your partner" for gendered words? Is it possible for the company to create a statement or additional handout to provide to employees to articulate why gender and sexuality are being provided and to guide them toward recognizing inclusion and lack thereof as they read? This is likely the least disruptive method of correcting the problem.

You may also wish to discuss with employees whether the health insurance policy is as inclusive as the needs of all employees. This may be handled via conversation, through anonymous surveys, or through deciding that insurance plans must include same sex partners, gender affirmation care, and adoption options for same sex couples. Work with leadership to discuss what can be done and offer to create or join a team to research viable options if there is not an obvious option easily available.

Scenario 12

Recently, your employee Jonathan has come out at medical facility as transgender. Jonathan has now asked to be called Tiffany and to utilize female pronouns. During a staff meeting, a leader keeps talking about this employee, using male pronouns, and calling the employee "Jonathan." When you ask the leader about this, the leader rolls their eyes and says, "Oh, you mean, 'Tiffany'?" and uses air quotes.

1. If you were the sole decision-maker at your medical facility, how would you choose for your medical facility to handle this situation?

2. Based on what you know of those in decision-making positions at your medical facility, what decision do you think they would make about how you must handle this situation?

3. Utilizing only your medical facility's employee handbook, what (if anything) do they dictate about how you must handle this situation?

4. If the answer to question #1 is different from the answers to question #2 and/ or question #3, what can you do, in your role in the medical facility? What (if anything) should you do?

SCENARIO 12.1

Would your answers be different if the employee had reached out to complain to you about the leader refusing to use the employee's correct name and pronouns? If so, how? If not, why not?

GUIDANCE

Having made it this far through this book, it is understandable that this employee's behavior is giving you pause. (Yay for you for recognizing a problematic situation that may not have caught your attention before beginning this book! *high five*) However, we don't know what this staff member knows about gender or about transgender people, so we do not yet know whether this behavior is due to intentional misgendering and inappropriate behavior or someone who currently lacks the knowledge necessary to understand what it means to have a transgender person in the medical facility and to understand appropriate responses to Tiffany both in her presence and out of her presence. Based on this, try to approach this employee privately. Explain that you weren't sure, based on their wording earlier, if they needed some support on the way to accepting Tiffany's name and gender pronouns.

(You can offer to share your copy of this book or recommend they purchase a copy. You can even offer to start a book club using this book and, later, other books on diversity.)

If the employee refuses or if the conversation with them indicates that they are aware yet intentionally misgendering Tiffany, speak with your supervisor. The goal is not to get someone in trouble; it is to protect Tiffany and other employees from being bullied by medical facility staff. Before reporting this to your supervisor, you may first need to ascertain the supervisor's level of career and knowledge on gender and transgender people. You can offer the same guidance and support to them as you did to the employee. The goal is to help guide and educate folks so that Tiffany and others are treated with respect, both by those who have gained a career and knowledge base and by those who recognize that not treating employees appropriately will lead to career ramifications.

Regarding Scenario 12.1, this indicates an ongoing problem that has become consistent enough that the employee complained. While you will need to follow your medical facility's protocol, you may wish to follow this situation more closely than more generalized complaints, as it may be necessary for medical facility staff with training to advocate for the employee and for inclusive policies and procedures. This can help prevent those without understanding from creating repercussions or medical facility protocols that can lead to unintended negative impacts on gender minorities within the medical facility. You can also provide support to the individual while they are in medical facility to ensure that they have a trusted colleague in the building.

Scenario 13

You are in charge of an office of employees, and you ask them to pair off to complete a training activity. As the employees separate into pairs, you notice that one employee, Jude, is being actively ignored by their peers. You decide to give the employees a moment to see if they self-correct, moving closer to listen in on what they are saying to one another. You hear them say that they won't partner with Jude because Jude is "weird." You do not know a lot about Jude, but you've been told by a leader in another office that Jude is "somewhere on the LGBT+ spectrum."

1. If you were the sole decision-maker at your medical facility, how would you choose for your medical facility to handle this situation?

2. Based on what you know of those in decision-making positions at your medical facility, what decision do you think they would make about how you must handle this situation?

3. Utilizing only your medical facility's employee handbook, what (if anything) do they dictate about how you must handle this situation?

4. If the answer to question #1 is different from the answers to question #2 and/ or question #3, what can you do, in your role in the medical facility? What (if anything) should you do?

GUIDANCE

Although the reasoning for Jude being ostracized is due to their being LGBT+, begin by treating this as you would any situation in which an employee is being left out. If those methods do not work, remind employees of the anti-bullying policies in your medical facility. Make a point to check in with Jude before or after a future meeting to find out whether further intervention is needed.

Once the immediate situation has calmed, reconsider your process for partner and group work. Rather than instructing employees to create their own, do this for them. This prevents any employee from being left out or feeling anxious about being asked to work with their peer(s). You may choose to assign employees at random, you could choose to use groupings based on birth month or favorite ice cream flavor or another arbitrary detail that all employees would have an opinion on, or you may wish to partner or group employees in ways that seem arbitrary but that encourage teamwork and ensure that employees who may learn from another's traits consistently interact with that person.

Next, ascertain whether the comments about Jude were a momentary and passing situation that has been solved by redirecting the employees or if this is an ongoing concern. Rather than lecturing during the meeting (likely causing employees to blame Jude for this), intentionally incorporate as much diversity into the office as possible. This may be focused on LGBT+ status, race, ethnicity, types of abilities, and so on. It may also be focused on all other types of differences and how differences are good for society and the industry you work within. For example, if you are dividing younger employees into groups based on their favorite ice cream flavor, take a moment to talk with younger employees about why it is good for the ice cream medical facility that people like different flavors and how it is easier to share if people do not want the same thing at the same time, since it means no one gives up their favorite. If employees are older, encourage them to consider how diverse learners may interpret the assignment differently or how coming from a different culture may lead to different results in a group work setting. Your goal is not to divert from your intended lesson plans, but rather to be intentionally and mindfully encouraging employees to think about all of the ways diversity exists around them. This will allow them to begin to view differences, to see how these can lead to benefits, and to be more open to positively considering their own uniqueness as well as that of their colleagues.

Scenario 14

After being at your medical facility for a number of years, you have become known for advocating for your company's medical facility to support many local organizations and events. This ranges from sponsoring little league teams to 5k charity runs. One day during lunch, a handful of employees approach, asking if you would support their written request for the company to sponsor a community event. They tell you it requires no effort on your part; they will handle the details; they just need to write your name down on the application form for company approval and get you to sign it. You agree. When they hand you the form for your signature, you find out that the community event is the city's LGBT+ Pride parade event.

1. If you were the sole decision-maker at your medical facility, how would you choose for your medical facility to handle this situation?

2. Based on what you know of those in decision-making positions at your medical facility, what decision do you think they would make about how you must handle this situation?

3. Utilizing only your medical facility's employee handbook, what (if anything) do they dictate about how you must handle this situation?

4. If the answer to question #1 is different from the answers to question #2 and/ or question #3, what can you do, in your role in the medical facility? What (if anything) should you do?

GUIDANCE

Depending on your medical facility, this may not even require any guidance! In many medical facilities, these organizational supports during Pride events have existed for many years without incident or concern. If your medical facility is open to this group—and since you have read this book—you are a great fit for this, and it sounds like your employees are excited to lead the process, so just continue to support them the way you do all of the other groups you've supported!

If your medical facility refuses the application to support a Pride event, work with the medical facility to find out their reasoning. Consider involving community leaders and the employee participants. You can also offer the medical facility information about other medical facilities in the news who refused to allow this type of group and the ways in which it became problematic to refuse, as well as the ways in which medical facilities can gain customers and community goodwill by participating.

If the sponsorship is ultimately approved, be sure to incorporate mindfulness when discussing the situation outside of the group wanting to start this sponsorship. Not every employee participant may identify as LGBT+, and it may not be safe for some to be assumed to. In addition, it is never okay for anyone to out another person, so it is crucial to have ongoing conversations with employees about how to speak up for what they believe is right without making choices that jeopardize their own or someone else's safety or career.

Scenario 15

Each month, your medical facility hosts a guest speaker. You are not sure who chooses the speaker or how the order is set; you simply know that you are tasked with being one of several staff members to sit in the auditorium and keep the employees quiet and seated during the presentation. At today's event, the guest speaker talks about the importance of family. As the person continues to talk, they begin to discuss the importance of having a mother and a father in the home. They stress that children growing up in homes without both mothers and fathers will grow up lacking life skills and they will always become a lesser quality person than their peers. When they give examples, the speaker talks about how girls should be learning to cook and keep the house from their mothers and boys should be growing up learning to mow the lawn and fix the car from their fathers. You know that there are employees and staff in the auditorium whose homes include same-sex parents, single parents, and parents who teach nontraditional roles to their employees.

1. If you were the sole decision-maker at your medical facility, how would you choose for your medical facility to handle this situation?

2. Based on what you know of those in decision-making positions at your medical facility, what decision do you think they would make about how you must handle this situation?

3. Utilizing only your medical facility's employee handbook, what (if anything) do they dictate about how you must handle this situation?

4. If the answer to question #1 is different from the answers to question #2 and/ or question #3, what can you do, in your role in the medical facility? What (if anything) should you do?

GUIDANCE

This situation may make you feel the need for immediate intervention. Some readers may already be envisioning themselves yelling out from the darkened auditorium, arguing with the speaker, making a rousing speech about inclusion, and the speaker leaving in a disgrace while the employees all cheer for inclusion. A great closing scene for a movie, no question, but this is not really realistic. Instead, consider the ramifications of letting the speaker finish and then addressing the situation as a medical facility. Maybe this means a medical facility-wide announcement that acknowledges that families are absolutely important and that families can look very different to the ones described by the speaker but that they are all equally valuable. Maybe this means you find ways to incorporate the value of different types of families and people into your lesson plans or meeting discussion for the next several days, to challenge the idea that a family can only look one way. Speak with your supervisor to ascertain whether the medical facility will be addressing this as a whole or whether you will need to speak to colleagues individually to share your concern and ask them to impart more inclusion in their offices to undo this narrow-mindedness on a smaller scale. Finally, talk with the medical facility to find out who chooses speakers and how the speakers are vetted before being chosen. Find out about creating a checklist of requirements in order to approve a speaker. You may even ask to be on the committee choosing or verifying speakers in order to ensure this does not happen again.

Scenario 16

Like many medical facilities, yours now has regular active shooter practice drills. You are new to the medical facility. Your role during these drills is to go to the cafeteria and guide the employees to a safe, less open space. This space has been designated to be the nearby bathrooms. As per the instructions, you are supposed to send the male employees into the men's bathroom and the female employees into the women's bathroom. Today is the first drill of this year, and it is the first time you have been assigned this role. During the drill, as you direct the employees, one employee points to another and says, "What about Dakota?" You remember that Dakota is transgender. While Dakota identifies as a woman, Dakota's medical facility records have a male designation. In addition to making a decision very quickly for the purpose of this drill, you also want to make the right decision and make a great first impression on your new boss.

1. If you were the sole decision-maker at your medical facility, how would you choose for your medical facility to handle this situation?

2. Based on what you know of those in decision-making positions at your medical facility, what decision do you think they would make about how you must handle this situation?

3. Utilizing only your medical facility's employee handbook, what (if anything) do they dictate about how you must handle this situation?

4. If the answer to question #1 is different from the answers to question #2 and/ or question #3, what can you do, in your role in the medical facility? What (if anything) should you do?

GUIDANCE

In an active shooter drill or a drill related to any safety concern, the sole goal is to keep all employees safe. While it is understandable that you want to do a good job for your supervisor, this is not about you. It is about safety. That's it. As such, all that matters is that every employee is brought into a bathroom during the drill. Since many transgender employees experience bullying in the workplace, it is important also to maintain Dakota's safety during the time spent in the bathroom. Your goal is to make it safe for every employee to go into the bathroom that matches their gender identity. This means that Dakota should be instructed to go with the women into the women's bathroom. If there is not an affirming and supportive staff member going to each bathroom, but there is the option for you to choose which to go into to sit with employees, go into the bathroom with the transgender employee any time there is a transgender employee involved. This helps to ensure their safety during the drill in case there is any cause for concern. As a result, all employees will be in the bathroom, per your duties to move them into these locations, and Dakota and any other current or future transgender employee(s) will be kept safe during the drill itself.

Once the drill is over, speak with your Supervisor about whether there is an existing policy for these situations in regard to transgender employees. If not, ask to write it or to be part of the group that writes it. If there is a policy and it is not inclusive, ask to rewrite it or be part of the group that rewrites it. If the policy is inclusive, encourage the supervisor to make sure all staff are aware of the policy so that there is no confusion or mistakes made in the event of a future drill or true emergency. You may even wish to include this information where you keep your employee roster and any emergency drill instructions so that you and anyone who may be with you during this time have easy access to this.

PUT YOUR KNOWLEDGE INTO PRACTICE

Section Summary

This section takes the foundational knowledge and the scenario hypotheticals and turns them into real-life action within your medical facility. While it is understood that the readers of this book work within a wide variety of professional roles, the intentions for this section are to allow you to become more mindful of the realities of your spaces and the information being disseminated to your medical facility's community so that you can make intentional decisions within the scope of your position to best support LGBT+ people.

How to Use This Section

Some portion will apply to all, regardless of their role within the workplace. Others are specific to individual job roles. You are encouraged to focus on the parts most applicable to your own role, while also being mindful of the recommendations and guidance that benefits your patients and/or their guests, colleagues, superiors, and those whom you supervise. While focusing on one's own scope of work is logical, understanding where there is opportunity to support others in areas outside of your particular role can allow for an overarching change within a workplace, and it allows folks to support one another as they advocate for transformations within their own professional roles.

DOI: 10.4324/9781003167303-19

Section Take-Away

This section offers the reader a way to assess their medical space's current inclusiveness, offers guidance on improving the physical space, policies, and protocols, and provides suggestions on alterations to create a supportive and affirming environment.

Chapter 12

Assessing Your Workplace

Although the previous sections may already have your mind swimming with ideas for change, before beginning to work to implement these ideas, it is vital to become mindful of all of the areas in need of change. Some readers may be reading this book individually, while others may be reading it as a leaders' cohort, an entire facility's staff, an all-insurance network or all-medical group mandate, or an entire industry collective. Whatever your individual experience, you may wish to seek out a trusted colleague or suggest working together as a small group of people at your workplace location to assess your individual and group practice, both so that there are a variety of opinions weighing in and so that there is already a contingent in place to begin the change process once the needs for change are fully recognized.

It can be easy to want to go back in time as far as possible when considering ways in which your medical facility could improve upon its inclusion practices. However, this can result in significant frustration of wishing things would have been done differently when the focus now should be what can be done differently today and what can be set up so that situations occur differently moving forward. With this in mind, decide to consider the past 1 or 2 years and do not become distracted by what has occurred in the facility before then, unless there's been a specific incident within your facility as well as within the laws related to medical mandates. It is possible that your workplace has not changed its ways significantly in the past 1 or 2 years, so this allows for the consideration of continuity rather than focusing on something that may have occurred only once for a specific need for one person, one team, or one office location.

First Impressions

Although it can be easy to want to jump right into the physical space itself, begin by considering the experience of patients, employees, and their families. Pretend that you are brand new to the facility. Obtain documents that would be provided

DOI: 10.4324/9781003167303-20

to new patient or employee. Think about what would be handed or e-mailed to them immediately upon their entrance (patient intake forms, hiring forms, etc.) and at patient discharge or the end of any probationary period. Examine those documents carefully with the new inclusive knowledge you have. How many gender-marker boxes are on the form? Is there a place on the form for a person whose name is not the same as the name on their birth certificate? How are the spaces worded for anywhere where children's names and genders are listed (such as health insurance requirements)? When legal documents cannot be altered by the facility (such as tax forms or insurance paperwork), is there a space on forms or an addendum option for gender inclusivity and to document the names the individual or individuals use, if these are not the same as on legal documentation? Are there any other areas on any of the forms that would indicate to an LGBT+ person that a patient or employee who identifies as such is anything less than fully welcome?

Hiring Processes

Now, look into the hiring processes of your department or entire facility. First, begin by researching where a job opening is posted. This may be something you can access directly, or it may require you to reach out to the human resources department. If the information is listed only on the facility or department's website, look at the website through the eyes of an LGBT+ person. Is there information on the website that indicates whether the organization is inclusive? Is there wording on the website that only engages people who fall into the gender binary? Are there photos or drawings of leaders or staff? Do those images depict different types and appearances of people? Now, review the job posting itself and other postings for other jobs. Are you seeing any wording that indicates whether or not the business or specific role is inclusive? Frequently, nondiscrimination policies are listed either at the bottom of individual job posts or somewhere in the job board section of the website. Do you see that? If so, is the language fully inclusive, containing protections for individuals regardless of sexual orientation and gender identity? If the job is posted in places other than on the facility's or medical group's website, where is it posted? If it is posted in public newspapers, websites, or magazines, take time to review those. Who is the audience for each? What are the images of people depicted in each? Does your community or city have a location-specific LGBT+ newspaper, magazine, or website? If so, does the facility post job openings there with the same frequency they post them to non-LGBT+ specific places?

Next, examine the job application process itself. Some organizations still require handwritten documents. If yours does, request to review one from the human resources department. (They are typically standard for all positions within the facility or medical group, with additional department-specific paperwork required.) If the job application process is electronic, review this instead. As sexuality is typically not questioned or documented on the majority of job application paperwork, review the documents as if you were a person whose gender identity does not match the information on their legal documentation, such as a birth certificate or Social Security card, documents that are required to prove identity when being hired. On the application paperwork, is there a gender-marker question? If so, how many options are available? Is there a place for an applicant to document that they use a name that is not the same as the name on their legal documents? Is there a place to document that their diploma, leadership license, or work experience was awarded to or occurred under a different name? As you review these, also look to see whether the electronic process, if there is one, allows an applicant to continue to complete the paperwork if they leave a question blank. In some cases, for example, where the available gender options are binary, a person may feel they have no choice but to leave that question blank if neither of the two options are applicable. However, if the computer program does not allow the applicant to continue applying without answering that question, this is important to note.

Next, try to speak with someone in the hiring department to find out whether the facility or entire medical group has any record of a transgender person or gender nonbinary applying. Find out if the hiring department receives any training in the event of such an applicant and how they would handle it if the name on legal documents does not match the name on the application. In places where staff are assigned an e-mail address that includes the person's name, find out if or how the human resources department would instruct the technology team to create an e-mail address for a person whose legal name and the name they use do not match. Also, ask what the process is to change that e-mail address in the event of a name change. It is likely that there is a procedure for this, as it is common for some married people to change or add to their last name. However, the information sought after here would be more aligned with the changing of a person's first name, as would occur in the event that a staff member began to use a different name that better aligned with their gender identity during the process of coming out and/or transitioning.

After Being Hired

Let's consider the experience for someone who has been enrolled in or hired at your facility or medical group.

First, let's focus on the time between when someone is hired and when they begin their work at their office, department, or position. Does your workplace have any sort of orientation for new employees? These typically occur for new employees, though they may also occur for an employee who has transferred from one location to another, whether within a medical group, traveling nurses, interns on various rotations, etc. The intentions for these are typically to have the employees tour the facility and interact with current employees who may be members of the workplace's leadership, the person's direct supervisor, and/or members of any team they may work on or colleagues they may be working near or on shifts with within the space. Examine any flyers or e-mails that are sent out to alert the intended participants to these orientations. Is all language inclusive to allow all types of people to know that they are welcome? It is important to review these documents for inclusive wording and policies.

Now, let's consider staff training or orientations. Is there a process for training or introducing new staff? If so, what is this process? Does this have mandated paperwork to complete? In some spaces, this is where new staff would complete paperwork regarding health insurance, which may list family members' names. In other cases, staff may complete emergency contact forms. If your business requires either, review those documents. In some cases, health insurance paperwork may be mandated by an insurance company or by the federal government. In these situations, the documents may not be able to be altered to become more inclusive. However, there is nothing to stop an organization from including a note in the paperwork packet to acknowledge that these forms are not fully inclusive and to articulate why the practice is unable to alter them to make them such. While this does not change the form, it does allow the individual to recognize that the leadership is aware of the problematic language and that they do not support this wording. On the emergency contact forms, how are the options worded there? Is the assumption that a person would be listing their spouse or their parents? Many LGBT+ people have someone else who knows them best and would best represent their wishes in the event of an emergency. In addition, it is possible that some would prefer to include information regarding anyone they do not wish to have contacted, even if that person may be considered their legal next of kin. Is this an option on the existing paperwork?

Obtain a copy of the agenda for any of these orientations. If there is paperwork that exists to train the person who gives these orientations or if there is paperwork that the person in this role uses, examine those as well. Are these documents preparing to welcome all types of employees? If this occurs in groups, do any prior written speeches or scripts or prerecorded trainings that include phrases such as "ladies and gentlemen," which would not include people whose gender is nonbinary? Are groups ever split based on gender?

During an orientation or introduction-to-colleagues experience for someone new to the staff, what information is preprepared? At some places, a name tag is already typed and waiting for each individual when they arrive. If yours offers this, where does the preparing person get this name information from? While this can be problematic for someone who does not use the name on their legal documents, this not only impacts those whose gender identity does not match; it can also impact people who prefer a shortened version of their first name, who go by their middle name, or who may otherwise want to begin their collegial relationships using the name they identify with.

The Written Rules

Now that we have new employees hired and oriented, let's take a look at what the organization has chosen to put in writing to address behavioral expectations.

Let's begin with the employee handbook. These are often sent to new employees and/or all employees in advance of the beginning of the business year. Review the nondiscrimination policy. Look into the wording of any anti-bullying and anti-harassment policies. Are there specific policies related to sexual orientation and gender identity? If there are policies spelled out for bullying based on race, religion, or other groups typically associated with hate crimes, it is important to note whether sexuality and gender are also included. Are restroom policies listed? Is there anything in the policy dictating which employees may use which restroom?

Next, look at the dress-code section. It is very common for dress-code sections to be divided by gender. Is yours? Is anything in the dress-code policy discriminatory, based on what you have learned about gender identity and gender expression? For example, is hair length mandated for male employees? Are there any rules listed about makeup being for female employees only or about male employees being prohibited from wearing skirts or dresses? Smaller medical facilities and independently owned nonfranchise practices may be able to quickly make alterations. Larger hospitals, medical groups, and practices with multiple locations may need to speak with a larger governing body in order to request changes that are either specific to your location or to advocate for facility-wide more inclusive changes to be made.

This should be considered carefully, and this part of the staff handbook should mandate how staff members are expected to respond when employees break a rule in the employee handbook. Is anything listed specifically on how to respond to an employee going through a gender transition? Is there anything specific listed on how to respond when an employee bullies or harasses a peer or a staff member for their sexual orientation or gender identity? Interactions with employee families may also be spelled out in this handbook. Is there anything listed regarding employees who are not accepting or affirming of an employee's sexual orientation or gender identity? This handbook may also list harassment policies between staff members. What is listed regarding the harassment of an employee based on their sexual orientation or gender identity? If this occurs, what do the handbooks say about how to report the situation and to whom? You may also want to find out if the person meant to receive that report has training that specifically includes sexual orientation and gender identity. Finally, this handbook may offer mandates or recommended guidance regarding how an office, office door, or other employee-facing space may be decorated. Are there any rules that would prohibit the inclusion of LGBT+ symbols or the symbols or acknowledgment of support of other minority groups?

Introduction into the Learning Environment

Now that you've completed a cursory overview of the information that would be provided to new employees, as well as the handbook for staff, you can begin to consider the patient experience itself. (If you are a leader who works within more than one location, you will want to do this for each building.)

Remember intersectionality here and be mindful to examine this for all patients, including those who may have different needs, such as employees in wheelchairs, employees who are hard of hearing or Deaf, and employees with developmental delays whose needs may be differently handled from those of the majority of employees. You may also need to assess private companies if your facility outsources translators or technology accessibility programs for some employees.

If possible, begin at the front doors of your office or wherever your patients enter the building each day, just as a patient would, envisioning the experience through their person's eyes. Walk through the halls and keep an eye open for anything that would indicate to them that this space and the medical care providers in it are inclusive and accepting. You may find this in terms of inclusive stickers on front doors, office doors, or waiting room walls. You may find this in wording on posters or within the information prominently displayed in the entryway, or by examining the way the medical organization interacts with the community based on the artwork or informational posters hung throughout the space. Are the employees or community interactions depicted in posters and pamphlets throughout the space inclusive of individuals of different races, gender identities, and abilities? If they include depictions of families, do they show families that have same-gender parents or single parents, or families in which the guardians are connected to the kids in some obvious other way (such as grandparents with kids)? If there is information about showing romantic pairs, do you see same-sex couples? If there are pamphlets or other marketing materials about how families can benefit from your products or services, are same-sex couples included? Are the words used within these materials gender-neutral?

Assessing Your Medical Facility

Let's consider restrooms. If you were a patient here whose gender identity does not match the gender they were assigned at birth, would you know which restroom you would be permitted to use? If there are multiple restroom options for those with varying gender identities, how far are they located from where a waiting room or treatment room may be? Is it realistic to expect a patient to be able to move from the furthest possible space to that restroom and back, both without missing a visit from a care provider and without being uniquely impacted by traveling long distances each time restroom use is needed, knowing they may be struggling with pain, trauma, and being in an unfamiliar location? Is this significantly different from the experience for patients whose gender assigned at birth aligns with their gender identity? Are there spaces in bathrooms for patients to have privacy? In family waiting rooms or rooms where bad news is delivered to patients' families, are different types of people depicted in the material of any products or services that are recommended? If so, are they depicted positively and equally to traditional family units? (This may range from drug companies' advertisements to recommendations for funeral services for those who need guidance on what to do after being told a loved one has died.)

Chapter 13

In the Medical Office and Collaborative Spaces

Beginning again with the patient's perspective, focus now on your space. Based on your role in the medical facility, this location may vary widely. For leaders, this may be your office. For others, this may be the standard cubicle or a nurses' station. For those who provide transportation, this may be the same vehicle each day or supplies you bring with you into each vehicle you use to transport patients. For other professionals, those whose work has them moving to the employees rather than having an office of their own, and those in the janitorial or kitchen staff, this space may be a supply cart, a section of a common area, or computer or skills or research lab; it may be your cafeteria line or your janitorial closet.

As you ascertain what areas or items to focus on for this section of the assessment, think about where you are most often found within your workday. Consider where employees or patients would find you if they were seeking you out and what you tend to be doing or carrying. The goal here is to become mindful of what message that space or item(s) may represent. Do you have any materials that show support of LGBT+ people? Are there areas where other beliefs or groups of people are shown? (This may be religious, it may be related to the clubs or groups your facility sponsors, it may be in relation to the pioneers of the subject matter you focus on, it may be your personal hero, it may be family photographs at your desk, etc.)

DOI: 10.4324/9781003167303-21

Chapter 14

Leadership and Learning Materials

In this section, since the focus of a medical career is always on patients, it can be assumed that supporting LGBT+ inclusion in the workplace supports everyone within that workspace. As such, there is no need to differentiate here for the perspectives of every level and type of patient. (Thus, this may be the most cost-effective, efficient, and impactful way to insert LGBT+ inclusion.)

While the legalities of name changes and using the names patients request staff to call them vary by city and state, if your workplace allows you to call "Jaclyn," "Jacky," or "Jay" if they request, it is logical that your facility (and/or you) ought to also support patients whose requested name is based in their gender identity. How is that name changed so that it appears correctly on all patients' engagement paperwork? While you will need to have a legal name for insurance purposes, the goal is to not have the patient called by their legal name or have to correct each care provider whom they meet. Think about and/or create a process so that the patient can provide the name they use once and every care provider has access to this and automatically uses it when addressing the patient or their loved ones.

Looking at your specific leadership tools can seem specific to your specialty or the role you have within the workplace. If your facility has mandatory readings or trainings (including textbooks, conference materials, internship work, continuing education work, supervisory worksheets, etc.), are LGBT+ people mentioned at all? Are there any areas in which LGBT+ people (real or simulated) are utilized? If so, are they depicted positively or negatively? For those whose job focus is administrative, consider your meetings on learning, employee enrichment, curriculum development, and all others that focus on how to better the employees' ongoing learning experience, as well as those that center on employment, staff retention, and continuing career/training for staff. Are there any that focus specifically on LGBT+ employees? Are there any that consider the needs of LGBT+ staff? How

DOI: 10.4324/9781003167303-22

many focus on providing guidance for ways to include more LGBT+ awareness or diversity, equity, and inclusion? For those whose job focuses on employee and staff interaction while providing food, medical supplies, janitorial, after-business, mentoring, or other services, do you receive any training for the specific needs of LGBT+ employees or staff? Also, are there trainings specific to the realization that intersectionality exists? For example, are there trainings and recognitions of the specific needs of Black transgender women or elder gay men or nonbinary immigrants?

Chapter 15

How to Implement Change

Once you have gathered documentation that recognizes the areas in which your medical community is already inclusive, as well as the areas in which there is minor or significant room for improvement, it is time to begin the process of creating and implementing those changes. For some readers, they may be in a position of enough power right this very moment to begin to draft these changes and submit them as new rules. For most readers, however, it may seem you are not in a position of power. As such, it can now feel as if you have become aware of problems but have no opportunity to solve them. Understandably, this can feel very frustrating. However, this does not have to be the case!

Now, you are likely looking at notes from information gathered during the assessment process and notes for how best to reach out to those in power positions to create and implement change. If this feels a bit overwhelming, that is okay! Certainly, if it were your job to make everything happen solely on your own, that would be very big job! However, this is very likely not the case. In fact, there may already be people who support creating a more inclusive and affirming environment. Maybe these are people who have also been required to read this book, if that is why you are reading it. Maybe these are people who employees have come to know they can trust and count on. Maybe these are other community leaders who frequently donate financially or in kind to various organizations and programs within your facility. In addition, you may not know how many patients, employees, and/or their family members identify as LGBT+ individuals and/or allies and supporters.

The first step is to take time to recognize who in your medical space or system does have a level of power, either to directly influence or by being in a position to join you in your goal promoting consideration for increased inclusion. This may be an elder who is well respected, it may be someone known for championing new programs within the organization, it may be founder, owner, or someone in a

C-suite position, it may be someone on the Board, or perhaps it is someone beloved by many regardless of their job title. Make a list of anyone who may be influential. Take time to think about the best way to approach each of these people. Some people may warm up best to casual conversation little bits at a time over a long period of time. Others may prefer a more formal sit-down meeting in which information is presented to them. Some may prefer to receive information or requests for support in writing via e-mail. By best understanding how to approach the people you want to buy into making your business more inclusive, you increase your odds of gaining their support.

Since you are reading this book, talking about it can be a great way to initiate these conversations in a casual way. You can begin discussing something you have read each time you bump into a person whose support you are seeking. Maybe you can share a fact, or maybe you prefer to share a thought or opinion you have about some part of the book. This can be a great way for conversation to occur organically, both about the information within this book and as a bridge to have conversations about the thoughts and feelings this book has brought up in you. These can be used to ask about a person's thoughts and feelings in response or reaction to yours. For those you think would prefer a more formal approach, either verbally or in writing, the notes you have made while assessing your workplace can become a great place to begin the conversation. Keep in mind that while you have become significantly more aware of areas of concern in which improvement can occur, unless everyone is mandated to read this book at the same time you have been reading, you will likely be talking to many whose understanding and awareness of the needs of LGBT+ people may be at or below the level yours was the moment before you began this book. It is vital to be mindful of this so that you offer foundational knowledge to someone unaware without coming across to them as patronizing. If this is not something you feel prepared to provide, you can always refer back to this book for guidance. You can either utilize language from the book as it was provided to you, or you can share the idea that the person you are speaking with may benefit from taking time to read this book by talking about the ways in which you feel you have benefitted from this reading experience.

Sample Scripts

Here are some sample scripts you can use to reach out to individuals in writing (typically done via e-mail or a facility's internal messaging program) to schedule a meeting to speak with them regarding ideas you have for areas of inclusion improvement:

■ I am reaching out to you after having read *The Medical Professional's Guide to LGBT+ Inclusion: Creating a Workplace Culture that Nurtures a Welcoming, Inclusive, and Affirming Environment.* As I read this book, I began to examine the ways in which our business is successfully supporting LGBT+ patients, families, and staff. I have also found some ways in which I know we can do better. I would love to schedule a time to talk with you about both. Please let me know when you are available to meet.

■ I wanted to reach out to you because I have begun to recognize that our medical facility is not as LGBT+ inclusive and affirming as it could be. I know that, as medical professionals, we pride ourselves in supporting the learning needs of all employees, and I would love to discuss ways we can be doing that better. When are you available to discuss this?

■ As we gear up to begin another month/semester/year at *MEDICAL FACILITY OR GROUP NAME HERE*, I have recognized that we have the opportunity to make some small but impactful changes that would support our LGBT+ patients, employees, and families. I would very much like to discuss these areas with you and to share ideas I have of how we can make these changes with minimal disruption to existing policies, procedures, and experiences for everyone. When do you have time to talk in the next week?

■ I am curious as to whether you have had a chance to read *The Medical Professional's Guide to LGBT+ Inclusion: Creating a Workplace Culture that Nurtures a Welcoming, Inclusive, and Affirming Environment* yet. I just completed it myself, and it highlighted for me where we are doing well affirming and supporting LGBT+ patients, families, and employees. I am so proud of us for those! It also helped me to recognize the areas in which we can improve. Let's schedule a time to discuss these!

Physical Space

Whether your space is an office, cubicle, cart, supply closet, cafeteria, or other space, small changes may be overlooked by many but will be noticed by those most in need of your support. If you are allowed to use decorations in your space, include images of LGBT+ flags. (Remember that there are a variety of flags indicating support for different people under the LGBT+ umbrella. These include the generalized rainbow flag as well as flags specific to transgender people, agender people, lesbians, bisexuals, pansexuals, and asexuals.) Anywhere your name is listed or written, you can add your pronouns. Typically, they go after your name or under your name and in parentheses. For example:

Harvey Polis (he/him)
Marsha Rivera (she/her)
Andrea Gilbert (they/them)

You can place this on your name tag on your staff mailbox, add it to your name on your door (if you have one), add it to any name tag or identification you wear while in the workplace, and anywhere your name is written.

If you supervise others, you may wish to begin this conversation by offering individuals the opportunity to give you information privately. To do this, consider offering a handout or sending an e-mail as an opportunity to get to know your employees, interns, etc. The short form may include questions such as

- How are you listed in the facility's directory? (Your full legal name)
- What name do you want me to call you?
- What pronouns do you use? (Circle all that apply)
  - She/Her
  - He/Him
  - They/Them
  - Ze/Zim
  - Other: _____
- Where may I use these pronouns? (Circle all that apply)
  - In meetings
  - With other staff
  - In communication with your emergency contact and family
- Would you like to meet with me privately to talk about this? (Circle)
  - Yes
  - No
- Is there anything else you would like me to know about your name or identity?

For those looking to simply share their own pronouns, they may choose in their e-mail signature, they may be listed as part of a staff list or facility website where all employees have access to office information, or, for those in other types of work, if your medical facility lists the cafeteria staff on the lunch menu handout and/or the janitorial staff on an office door or e-mail, that is also a place where pronouns can be included. This does not cost any time or money and will likely be ignored by most people. However, those whose pronouns do not match the gender they were assigned at birth or the gender that correlates with their appearance will notice. This is an unspoken acknowledgment that it is safe for them to share their pronouns with you. In other cases, some may notice and inquire. This is an opportunity for you to explain that not everyone's pronouns match the gender they were assigned at birth or their appearance. By explaining this in a matter-of-fact tone, you provide information without judgment and offer them the space to ask additional questions. If you would like to be even more upfront about this, you can include this when you begin meetings and any time you introduce yourself by including your name and your pronouns. In gatherings with those whom you do not work with often, at the time that you would typically ask employees to let you know if you are mispronouncing their name or if they go by something else or ask them to go around the room and introduce themselves using their name and their pronouns. (As a note, many people with names of non-white people or immigrants experience microaggressions when white Americans claim that the name is too difficult to pronounce and ask to call them a shortened or Americanized version of the name. Do not do this. Even if you need to ask them privately to speak their name slowly or a few times or asking them to write it phonetically, you do not get to make someone else uncomfortable so you can be comfortable.) When discussing names and pronouns, it may mean that you first need to explain what you are asking for and why. You should then set the example. You can give your name and pronouns to show them what this process is. (For example, "I will demonstrate by going first. I am Mr. Brooks, he/him" or "I will demonstrate, I am Mr. Brooks, I use he/him pronouns.")

Inclusive Curricula and Printed Training Materials

While many of us wish it were possible to either do away with current training manuals or industry standard protocols or swap them out for books filled with inclusivity and affirmation, this can be cost-prohibitive. In addition, as many training programs must utilize the same materials for years or decades, a change to the materials would require significant amounts of work on the part of the leaders as training programming, slides, and other documents would all need to change in order to support and supplement these materials. This can be unrealistic for many, and it can put an undue burden on training leaders who are already frequently overworked. As such, until the time when your facility is considering or planning to replace/update their materials anyway (at which time advocating for inclusive materials is vital), it is important to discern how to take existing materials and texts and make them more inclusive. The goal is inclusivity, but the secondary goals are to make changes that require little to no time, effort, or supplies. This makes the change as seamless as possible without adding stress onto training leaders.

In Closing

There has long been a saying, "Nice guys finish last." Typically, it is intended to mean that the only way to get ahead in life is to not be so nice. However, the reason others often finish first is not that they are not nice or unkind or even ruthless but because they have the support of others. If you pause for a moment to think about it, it is likely that you'll be able to think of people in almost any industry who gained seniority due to nepotism. You can also likely think of others who succeeded because they had mentors who guided them, wrote letters of recommendation for them, were professional references, or offered to introduce them to someone who was in a position to offer them work or other valuable professional information. It is incredibly likely that most or all of the examples you've known were white and male. It is likely that all of the examples you thought of were heterosexual and cisgender.

"Old boys clubs" are not a new concept. Many movies have depicted scenes of them within various professional industries. Often, they are shown at golf courses, in smoking rooms, over drinks in bars, or on vacations together. Although these appear to be social in nature, they are often also how friendships and partnerships are founded and reaffirmed. As a result, those who are invited to participate in these experiences are more likely to succeed than others. For decades, women have been working to succeed in spite of being kept from these bonding rituals. After many years, social clubs and networking events specifically for women are becoming more common. It is most common for these groups to be primarily heterosexual and cisgender. However, most leaders of most companies remain white, male, cisgender, and heterosexual. What about LGBT+ people?

In addition to often living in states and cities where an LGBT+ person can be mistreated with microaggressions for being LGBT+, these individuals are also fighting for the opportunity to succeed professionally, just like everyone. However, LGBT+ people are too often kept out of conversations, resulting in fewer opportunities to succeed not because of their talents or abilities but because of their lack of access to the same elite that others can access due to their backgrounds or upbringing or because a straight cisgender leader sees themselves in a subordinate. In some cases, LGBT+ employees, especially those who also identify as women, experience

DOI: 10.4324/9781003167303-24

finding themselves on a glass cliff. This is the term created by Michelle K. Ryan and Alexander Haslam that acknowledges the occurrence of when a failing or struggling medical promotes a woman or an LGBT+ person into a leadership role during times of significant stress. This is problematic because it sets the individual up for failure. Some may wonder why the person would take this job.

Unfortunately, many may only get this type of opportunity to lead. In other cases, a person may not know about the medical professional's identity because that insider information was not shared outside of the boys' club they do not fit into. In either case, the person entering the role is at a higher chance of failure, not because they are not qualified or capable but because the system and the support around that role is floundering. Much like the well-known often discussed glass ceiling, this situation highlights the inequities faced by members of marginalized communities within the medical world.

However, it does not have to be this way. Employees of an LGBT+ supervisor can work to support their leadership rather than to contribute to the person's struggle. C-suite leaders can be intentional not just in how the company hires its LGBT+ employees but also how the individuals are trained, mentored, and guided toward professional success. Every staff member regardless of their seniority can be active in their allyship in the workplace, helping to reduce or eliminate workplace bullying, harassment, and discrimination.

In a world where "nice guys finish last," it is incumbent upon every current and future medical leader to consider whether their own actions or inactions are causing some members of their team to struggle, to be more easily ignored, or to be less often positioned for success. After reading this book, it is the author's hope that you consistently revisit these insights, consider your privileges, identify your allyship opportunities, become more aware of your newly opened mind, and recognize your position within your industry. With these insights, may you take every opportunity to better support LGBT+ people in your professional community, from the hiring process to the employee's success in your industry and excel in your field as a leader to all, not just to some.

Afterword Written by Danny Roberts, Star of MTV's *The Real World: New Orleans*

Danny Roberts was once aptly described by Advocate Magazine as an "accidental activ-ist" after his appearance on the 9th season of MTV's "Real World: New Orleans." He is known as an LGBT+ pop culture icon and advocate of the early 2000s. His personal story, which included a highly publicized relationship with an army captain in the days of "Don't Ask, Don't Tell," is a touchstone for many in the LGBT+ community through their own coming out journeys. Through viewing his story each week, millions of Americans saw the real-life implications and experiences of this (now-overturned) bigoted military rule and the ways in which it impacted individuals in their daily lives. In addition, Danny's roots in a small town in the mountains of North Georgia, allowed Americans outside major cities to see that gay people exist in their communities too. This helped to open doors (and closets) to so many who thought they were the only one in their neighborhood. Danny's easy-to-love personality on-screen also helped soften the hearts and open the minds of millions who, before meeting him via television, thought they had never known a gay person.

Danny has spent the greater portion of his adult life living in Seattle and New York City after completing his degree at the University of Georgia in Athens. He's now the father of a young daughter and spends much of his time living in rural Vermont, work-ing towards his goal of living sustainably off the grid and running a hospitality business for guests seeking unique getaways. He is also a talent recruiter for tech startups and a career coach. Although his return to television in 2022 via "Real World Homecoming" re-introduced him to America, much of his story and medical journey has remained untold … until now.

DOI: 10.4324/9781003167303-25

I grew up in a small, fairly isolated town in the Appalachian foothills of Northwest Georgia. At my birth, my dad was a young long-haul truck driver who had met my mom and struck up a romance while regularly passing through my hometown with work. She was a server in a cafe where they met, both very young, but my dad clearly charmed and won her over. I arrived unexpectedly not too long later, and with that realization, they married. As you can see, my life began with humble blue-collar roots, and I was raised by extremely young parents. They remain married to this day and are genuinely in love, but it was by no means a Norman Rockwell family life ... more like a roller coaster. My mom soon put herself through college and got her nursing degree, ultimately working through my upbringing as an emergency nurse. Two brothers arrived later; one 3 years younger than me; the youngest is 9 years younger than me (later in life, he came out to the family as well). My parents worked long hours and we would often go days without seeing one or the other since my dad was on the road and my mom was often working late into the night. I became the de-facto parent much of the time as I moved into my teen years and was regularly tasked with watching after my brothers.

As kids, we had very little media exposure, quite the opposite to how children grow up today. My town was not wired for cable to the outside world until I was about 15 years old, so for most of my life, we had a few basic network channels. (And of course, the internet wasn't widely available until I reached college.) Though the world is far more wired today than it was then, we should remain aware that even currently, people across the country have wildly different levels of access to media and information, which is especially true the further back in time we go.

Having grown up in the rural south, being homosexual was seen as shameful and looked down upon, being viewed as an illness and moral defect to overcome. There were no overt examples of it I saw in popular culture, at least that were recognizable to a child and any rare mention around the subject of sexual identity was incredibly negative, so I lacked the tools to genuinely understand what different sexual orientations were or to describe my feelings. There was no other option than being hetero. End of story. Any diversion from the evangelical Christian mainstream understanding of sexual identity and gender roles was understood to be a moral failure. Hearing solely this negative framework through my childhood meant that I lacked understanding the concepts that applied to my own personal development, which I was working diligently and subconsciously to repress. The natural urges and inclinations blossomed in spite of those efforts to quash them, which I tucked away in the back of my mind and ignored. For the most part, it was not an active fight against myself. Rather, it was more of a passive process of unconscious repression. My primal brain understood that being homosexual was something far too dangerous to admit or embrace.

In school, I was more of a quiet kid who kept a handful of close friends but was not highly social. Though I was more curious than average and generally enjoyed my elementary and to a lesser degree, middle school years, by high school I was growing numb to the mediocrity of my school system and disengaged from much of my class time. I was known as the kid who regularly slept through half my classes, mostly taught myself what I needed to know, and still made decent grades. My high school wasn't exactly a competitive bastion of advanced learning, so mediocre effort did the job well to earn a college prep diploma. However, I excelled outside the classroom. I played tennis and competed on the academic team through high school. I was also a Cub Scout and Boy Scout, which was highly formative for me in multiple ways. It's where my love of the outdoors and environmentalism really took root, which carries on today. (It's also where some of my first exposure to homo relations between teen boys happened.)

I was actually having my first gay experience from around 15 to 17, though at the time I absolutely did not see it as homosexual. One of my closest friends and I had something that was ongoing—not a relationship, but a secret sexual entanglement which always revolved around basketball, video games, and camping. Some of it was also rooted in the Boy Scouts. Even though I was absolutely having a gay experience through that period, in my juvenile and terrified mind, I completely justified it as just us being aroused teenagers doing what we needed to do to get our first kicks, always setting the veneer of heterosexual boundaries. That meant that the practice was always purely functional in the pursuit of orgasm, never involved penetration, or most importantly, never had an emotional layer to it. (I'm still good friends with him to this day and he identifies as heterosexual. We have since acknowledged as adults what happened then.)

So that was my first guy, my first men who have sex with men (MLM) sexual experience. But even then, I justified it in my mind. It was driven out of natural human biological urges, but also very much psychological urges. I justified it with the most illogical logic and refused to think of it as being anything queer whatsoever. What I wasn't able to process at the time was that I absolutely ended up with an emotional component of our exploration—what I now recognize as an adult was that was my first heartbreak. As we got later into our high school years, his attention turned entirely to women, and with his first girlfriend, our sexual exploration ended. There was a part of me that celebrated that for him because I felt it was something we both should be moving toward. But another part of me was completely crushed. However, I could not and would not allow myself to accept that. I was so subconsciously hurt that I steered hard away from seeking anything with men until years later at university.

Around that same time, at about age 17, Red Cross came to collect blood and the friends I played basketball with and I all volunteered to donate. It should be noted that this is when the AIDS crisis was in full swing and the most widely held view was that HIV was a "gay disease." I was highly aware of and paid close attention to what I heard in my community and what the media narrative was around queer people. For instance, I was aware that gay men were not donate blood. (20+ years later, this is still true and still based on bias not science.) At that moment though, all I knew was that gay men could not donate and that I felt a strong urge to test the water to see how an adult would react if I revealed myself as homosexual.

Part of the nurse's job before collecting blood was to ask males if they've had sex with other men in order to select out homosexual donation. I drummed up the courage and said that I had, just to see her reaction. She absolutely lost her mind and reacted incredibly improperly for a nurse by vocally berating me! It was clear from her words that she did not think highly of homos and did not withhold her disgust. I admitted to the nurse that I was joking (she didn't find it amusing) and carried on with the process of donating, but that was the final external confirmation that my mind needed that being homosexual was something I would never embrace, no matter what I felt inside. For the next couple of years, any same-sex thought that popped in my head was actively stomped out.

As soon as I graduated high school, I was eager to leave my small town and its limited world view behind and did so that summer of 1995 when I left for the University of Georgia. It was there in Athens, Georgia, where I first began to expand into the person I am today. Most of my inner world had been kept highly repressed and tucked into the recesses of mind growing up. But college opened my eyes, mind, and heart to the capacity of this world and its people, leading me to cautiously accept that I had been avoiding major facets of my being. In addition, technology was advancing and my gaining access to the internet helped me to push boundaries and explore my curiosities in ways that had previously been impossible. Particularly, the ability to covertly explore my sexuality through safe online conversations played an enormous role in the early adulthood years. By the time I reached my final year of University, I had my first official boyfriend, I identified as bisexual, and I was open about it with those in my closest circle. By the time I completed college and began my first job, I had quietly admitted to myself that living a life as a lie was no longer an option for me.

As previously mentioned, my mom was an emergency nurse, and, as is true for many college students, I remained on her insurance during my college years. At around age 20, I needed to see a doctor. (The reason wasn't serious enough to remember but the resulting experience is.) My mom set the appointment up with a doctor that was in a practice tied to the hospital where she worked. This doctor happened to be someone she knew fairly well from their medical practice together. I went in to see him without thinking twice, absolutely assuming we had a degree of confidentiality and that whatever I shared with him was going to be treated as doctor-patient privilege. However, what transpired was the opposite of my naive assumptions.

As a part of his medical intake, he asked me about my sex life. I shared with him that yes, I had both active male and female sexual relationships. I'll never forget this in my life, the doctor just froze for a moment with a glazed look on his face. He attempted to stumble through the next couple of questions but paused and returned to the earlier statement about my sex life. Then he said, "listen, I really respect your mom. I want nothing but the best for her, and of course the best for anyone she cares for, especially all of her children. I really want you to think care-fully about what you're doing right now. The ramifications. Really want you to rethink this. Your lifestyle is dangerous and self-destructive." Stunned, all I could muster was, "excuse … me?" That moment of shaming is forever burned into my memory. Unfortunately, I was too stunned to really respond while trying to process his judgment and boundary crossing. His lecture came from a place of genuine care from his moral perspective, but I left there that day knowing that what happened was wrong. That event crushed my trust in medical practitioners for many years forward. The reality that was most terrifying to me wasn't that this doctor had judged and scolded me, it was that our conversation was not going to be privileged information after all. I had zero doubt he would be sharing this information with my mother and I waited in terror for my parents to drop me from their insurance. I don't know if that ultimately happened or not. My mom's the type that she could have been told the truth but perhaps blocked it out. All I know is that she did not speak a word of it; whether this was because she was never told or because she was in denial and self-preservation mode, I'll never know.

At a young age where you're already working hard to ground yourself in what you genuinely feel, hearing rejection and scorn from a trusted figure absolutely undermines the confidence you're trying to build and immediately makes you take two steps back. Even logically knowing that what had happened was very wrong made no difference. I went into an anxiety tailspin for weeks, worrying what I was going to hear from my parents. I was mostly independent when I left home, but still depended on my family in some small financial ways to help with living costs through school so I braced myself for really being on my own from then on, not to mention the possible broken relational ties. It was years before I came out to another medical professional.

Through most of my twenties, I never truthfully shared my sex history or iden-tity with health care providers who attended to me, whether it was routine care, emergency care, or even with my dentist. During each of my different interactions with healthcare providers for various reasons, I would never genuinely answer that question. I turned to a physician who was already a trusted close friend through most of my twenties for medical advice and opinion, though we lived nowhere near one another. As he was the only provider I felt safe with, I would actually save up and fly to see him occasionally for my medical needs.

Simultaneously, I graduated college with a degree in French and studied Foreign Language Education with the intention of teaching. However, at the end of my program and student teaching, I knew deep down that I was still far too young and immature to succeed in a classroom setting. As such, when I graduated in the Fall of 1999, I had no clue what I was doing next with my life. At that same time, a friend of mine encouraged me to attend an open casting call for the next season of MTV's *The Real World*, which I thought was absurd. The network was casting for the upcoming ninth season and it was a wildly popular show—a pop culture zeitgeist of its time. Yet I had seen very little of it over the years due to lack access to cable television. However, I had nothing to lose so I went and eventually learned from casting that I was essentially a shoe-in from the first time we all met. I saw it as a golden opportunity to publicly come out, to be forced to own my true identity once and for all.

Coming out on the show was also my catalyst to come out to my family, who by then had become highly involved as Evangelical Christians. One of my main motivators to do the show was the ability to vocally and visibly stop living a lie, particularly with my family and those close to me. Speaking my truth on national television was my way of holding myself as accountable as possible in spite of my fears of their negative reactions and possible broken ties. It felt a bit like having a fear of heights and being asked to jump from a plane but needing a push over the edge. I knew that there would be no going back.

Coming out to my family was not positively accepted. I prepared myself for the worst reactions possible, but their reaction was mostly void of any reaction. There was a veneer of begrudging acceptance, but in reality it was "I cannot deal with this so the easiest and safest thing for me to do is put on a smile to your face. But in reality, I'm going to pray for you and pray that you change." The longer life has gone on and the older and more attune I've become, that lack of acceptance has ultimately been the guardrail which guides the direction of our relationship. When I was younger, I was much more open and gave space to the idea that they would grow as humans with time, understanding, observation, and wisdom. I believed that they would watch me grow as an adult, come to recognize and respect what I've accomplished and then accept who I genuinely am. But the truth is, there's always been too much shame in the way of us having a close and mutual bond. To be really honest, that shame has just grown and metastasized because, in order to continue to build my own life, I have had to tuck that in a suitcase, trying to be suffocate it, but the feelings of abandonment and judgment by those I love most have never gone away. Sadly, I have reached the point in my adult life where I have lost patience for false peace. Instead, it's become incredibly important to me now to focus my energy on relationships where it's a give and take and we're being genuine with each other, and we have a baseline of human respect. Whether you are a loved one or a medical provider, if you sincerely believe there is something fundamentally wrong with me, it's incredibly difficult to be in that sort of toxic relationship with you without feeling a consistent degree of covert dismissal and disappointment.

Although I didn't have my biological family's support, I experienced so much support from the LGBT+ community as my story aired on MTV. While I never intended to be so impactful, I began to hear so many stories of kids and adults who came out, people who reconsidered their judgment of gay people, and those whose views became much more inclusive all because they saw my story. Though nothing replaces familial acceptance, certainly being seen and validated by anyone is impactful, especially on such a big scale.

After the show finished airing, my temporary fame eventually faded, and I returned to my regular life as a regular person in the world. I later married and spent 10 years with a partner with whom I adopted a child at birth. The year that we adopted her from Texas, Google released some national data that painted a clear picture of hate language being used on the web and where it originated. The town where Naiya was born and where her mom lives came up with some of the most homophobic, most misogynistic, and the most anti-Hispanic Google hate-speech ratings that year. We were nervous going to the hospital and just having to be—for the first time—absolutely upfront and open with so many strangers with power in their hands. There was no dancing around the fact that a gay couple was there to adopt an infant. The nurses were all great, except one of the night nurses. It wasn't standard practice for someone who at that point didn't have a legal claim to a child yet to go in to see them; however, the legal process takes time after the baby's birth. There's a few days of legal limbo during this time regarding who has rights and access to the baby and because Texas law didn't have any sort of recognition of scenarios like ours where we had no legal claim, this night nurse would not allow us to hold our new baby nor to feed her through the night. This night nurse knew our story, the other nurses had explained it during shift change. We genuinely felt was that this woman had a moral problem with two gay men adopting this baby and she was going to intercede in any way she could using the only power she had—to keep us away from our baby during the entirety of her shift. She was cold about it. The next morning when the next nurse came, she was so unapologetic for what happened that night, gave everybody a cold stare, and walked away. This was the moment I thought to myself, "oh boy, is this what we're going to be regularly up against?"

It is also worth mentioning that this could have been a much longer time of legal quagmire due to the legalities of who could have requested or provided medical care to our new baby had an emergency occurred. Though at the time we were legally married in Washington State, same-sex marriage wasn't then federally recognized, so states didn't have to recognize it either thus Texas did not recognize us as a married couple. To legally adopt her, one of us had to adopt her first and then re-adopt to add the other as a primary caretaker. We had to do the adoption twice because there was no legal route to adopt her as two "unmarried individuals," as the state laws unfortunately viewed us. Luckily, our baby had no medical emergencies during this time, though I can only imagine how that night nurse might have treated us if something would have occurred during the time when only one of us had legally adopted her and the other was still in process.

Being same-gender parents can take on its own set of stigma and challenges, especially when seeking medical care for her throughout her life. After the past twenty years of living in cities such as Atlanta, New York, and Seattle, we chose to raise her in rural Vermont. As such, I have been readjusting to a different level of awareness in what people accept as objective reality; being forced to recognize that the lives that people experience growing up and living in urban and suburban areas is wildly different from those of rural America. While this could have been really scary or difficult, I'm grateful that, for our family, the medical system we use in New England where we live has a progressive intake and approach that is confirming and open to nontraditional families and scenarios. It seems to be the philosophical norm with their approach. Plus, though we are no longer a couple, we always try to take our daughter together, so it's an obvious same-sex parenting unit.

There are challenges to be being a gay dad in particular that I had not originally foreseen but which society points out to me often. Society still views caretaking as more of a female role. With that said, many mothers to hold the same views and identify closely with that role. Most literature, tools, advice, support groups, and so on, including those offered by medical professionals in pamphlets, support groups, and training events are still geared toward women. Plus, since heterosexual fathers are often in more traditional roles and thus often much less involved in some aspects of parenting and child socializing, there's often an outsider awkwardness of being the sole dad hanging out with moms at the playground. While LGBT+ people are often thought to be one group, the divide between gay dads and lesbian moms is also very present for us. This is because it can still feel alienating to attempt to break into the inner world of that special mom bond that happens between women with their children. On the flipside, as most gay men don't have children, most lack much or any concept of what is involved in parenting as it is not part of their life whatsoever. In cases of hetero parents with involved fathers, often living culturally distinct lives creates a divide between us. When I'm with other parents, often time, our only commonality is the fact that we have children. It can feel a bit isolating at times. I don't think this is true for all LGBT+ parents, but I suspect it's the case with the majority. Too often, well-meaning medical professionals do not consider this when encouraging gay parents to join parenting groups or to sign up for classes with their babies.

Location likely makes a huge difference here. The larger and denser the city you live in, the likelihood of there being other LGBT+ parents in your community to bond with, or at the very least more hetero parents who may live in unique, nontraditional family arrangements themselves are more likely. In all honesty, I had no clue what being a gay dad was going to feel like as I didn't know a single LGBT+ identifying person who had a child. Now being a parent is very natural, just a part of my existence and being, but I think that took time to develop. I think for a lot of LGBT+ people particularly, we have to spend so much of our energy and life force discovering and embracing our true selves, rejecting and excising what has been projected on to us, building confidence in ourselves, and learning to do all of that within a hetero world and framework that we are exhausted in ways others do not understand. When you're actually required to shift the majority of your energy to focusing on another human being for survival, I think it's a drastic shift for a lot of us. Working with doctors for Naiya's care who have some sense of these unique challenges we face as LGBT+ parents, understanding that we may not have a wide net of support behind us, yet encouraging us and approaching us with a radically equal degree of respect is likely the most affirming and care we could ever ask for.

As someone with a child, I know I have more to live for than just myself and thus the focus on my health has become an even higher priority to me. In my mid-30s, I finally started seeing a regular provider whom I felt safe to be honest with. In order to obtain this safe experience, I specifically chose to find and have a gay doctor. It's a comfort level where I never hesitate or second guess what I'm sharing. He prods me to think about things that he is aware of in the community that I should know about, whereas someone who's not living the day-to-day life is getting their data second hand and they're possibly interpreting it however they chose. If I were seeking a new care provider today, as someone much more comfortable and public in my identity, having a gay doctor wouldn't be an absolute requirement; I don't mind seeing doctors who don't identify as LGBT+ when it's necessary. However, after that first horrible experience, I still prefer my main medical point of contact to be gay and to specialize in HIV care. (This is because I am HIV+.) I need to know that my provider is genuinely accepting of who I am and that they prioritize being very up-to-date on cutting-edge research, treatments, and experiences tied into being HIV+.

When I think about my life as a whole, I have experienced some of the least affirming and most affirming medical care. I have had my life scrutinized and judged, had my newborn daughter withheld, and feared being outed by medical professionals. I have also had providers who have listened, who have affirmed me, who have celebrated the birth and milestones of my child with me, and who have worked with me as a team to ensure that my family receives consistent supportive care no matter our medical needs. *The Medical Professional's Guide to LGBT+ Inclusion: Creating a Workplace Culture that Nurtures a Welcoming, Inclusive, and Affirming Environment* may seem like a book intended to target a niche population. However, there are LGBT+ patients everywhere, including those who are out and proud and those who think they will never come out. Affirming care not only impacts us within the LGBT+ community, it impacts those who love us. Certainly, I benefit from my health but so does my daughter, a young vibrant girl who I hope never has to grow up and worry about whether either of her fathers get treated with respect and top medical care. The world is filled with politics, with religion, with struggles. This book helps to ensure that no patient is mistreated due to someone else's views, and it celebrates the Hippocratic Oath to not only heal but to do no harm.

Appendix I: Opposition

Although this book is intended to be useful, guiding, and inspiring, it would be unwise to pretend there is no chance of opposition in response to the goals and efforts of making spaces and office materials more LGBT+ inclusive. By recognizing this as possible, we can better prepare for the situation if and when it occurs. This allows for a calm and intentional response, rather than an off-the-cuff remark or statement made in anger which could become more combative than helpful in moving equality forward within your medical facility.

Let's take a look at the stakeholders and where their opposition may stem from and how to respond to it.

Community Leaders (Including C-Suite and Board Members)

Depending on the area, those in powerful positions may have little or no direct involvement with your employees. They may also spend their time managing political expectations and aspirations, writing policies and procedures, and/or otherwise basing their work on many aspects of the requirements of their role that are not necessarily aligned with the realities of on-ground experiences and needs. This is typically not an intentional disconnect, but rather an unfortunate byproduct of overworked individuals trying to juggle a variety of responsibilities and decisions without enough time to regularly engage with those who work in the medical facilities.

If opposition happens here, begin from a place of offering guidance. Perhaps the concern is that making room for LGBT+ inclusion means undermining the current goings-on of the facility. Perhaps the concern is that adding LGBT+ inclusion means lessening the focus on areas where sales or other numbers require high employee numbers or patient satisfaction in order to continue to receive funding or to meet specific goals mandated to them either by a franchise board or by previously set annual or quarterly expectations. Before responding to the complaint, clarify what the person is afraid of. This will allow you to respond to their anxieties. It may be helpful to recommend a copy of this book to offer them the foundational knowledge that may provide them with enough understanding to recognize the importance of LGBT+ inclusion in medical facilities. It may be helpful to offer them the most recent studies on LGBT+ adults bullying and suicidality. It may also be helpful to offer to show them ways in which you are incorporating LGBT+ inclusion and affirmation into your office or medical building without it costing time or money. This way, either you can end their apprehension, or you can know that the stress comes not from a lack of knowledge but from a difference of opinion and priorities.

While there is not always a way to convince top leaders to understand and appreciate the ways in which adding in conversations about diversity, equity, and inclusion benefits employees, by framing the focus on the benefits of employee mental health, by tying it to the most recent studies on bullying and suicidality, and by showing how the addition does not take away from the previously determined professional goals, you are most likely to at least calm them enough to avoid opposition that attempts to remove LGBT+ inclusion from the list of overarching plans and goals. Over time, as they see that budgets and work productivity do not change, they may become less interested in whether or not LGBT+ inclusion occurs. Over more time, as they see that, in addition to no negativity, mental health improves or the suicidality rates in the medical spaces do not increase, they may even come on board to support the inclusive changes.

Medical Leaders (Including Supervisors and Department Heads)

Commonly, people in these roles have to walk a line between supporting their employees and answering to their supervisors. This can place them in precarious positions, especially when a medical facility is working to make changes that can cause waves to start within both groups of people. Often, if their supervisors are supportive of LGBT+ programming, employees will get on board, if only because they do not feel it appropriate to second-guess or argue with their bosses. In some cases, when many employees are supportive of LGBT+ programming, the leaders can ascertain that this offers enough vocal support of the change that it can lead the community leaders to become more open to ideas or more supportive of them. By understanding which side is struggling with this planned change, a person can better assess the hesitation in the medical leader(s) at their own medical facility.

In some cases, medical leaders struggle with the responsibility of overseeing the numerous changes within their physical spaces. If this is the case, offer to assist. This may be by looking into more inclusive images for the facility's walls and their website. This may be rooted in working with colleagues to review and amend lesson plans. This may be in offering ongoing support to the concerned person through the change process or through offering ongoing auditing and revision of LGBT+ inclusion at regular intervals throughout one or more years. Find out where the frustration or dread is coming from and do what you are capable of to tackle tasks or provide support.

Company Employees

Often, opposition from employees occurs when it appears that new programs or policies will result in an increased workload to those who are already over-worked. It can be easy for them to envision being forced to rewrite every training manual, to redo every office, and to change every way in which they have been working for the number of years they have been contributing to the success of employees in your medical facility. This opposition happens frequently because increased workload often occurs. As such, it is no wonder that some in your medi-cal staff may have an immediate negative reaction to word that LGBT+ inclusion is beginning! Luckily, though, this can be an easy problem to overcome.

First, recommend this book so that they can utilize the same foundational knowledge that you now have. This can help them to understand why LGBT+ inclusion matters. Next, guide them to see how little has to change from their cur-rent practices. For example, asking employees their pronouns costs no money and takes only a moment longer during a meeting where people are sharing their names before the meeting begins. Offer to take time to walk through some of their current practices with them to provide guidance on how to incorporate more LGBT+ fig-ures and topics without making any significant changes to the plans and materials that have worked well for them and that have been well received by their employees. You can even refer them to the section in this book that fits their focus area, where they can do a quick read to gather ideas. This can help get them thinking while also reinforcing that no one is expecting them to scrap everything and start over. This ought to lessen the anxieties and stress that many may have felt when they found out there were changes coming to the medical practice, without having recognized the minimal amount of effort it would require of them to make those changes in their work.

The other common reason for opposition from staff is one of an argument that LGBT+ people/behaviors/issues go against their personal beliefs. This may be stated as being religiously based, and it may come from the way they were raised; it may be rooted in their culture. While the goal is never to make a person feel uncomfortable in the workplace, it is vital that medical leadership at all levels be mindful of inclu-sion and equal treatment for all, regardless of the personal beliefs. It may be helpful for those with these concerns to utilize the internet to search for support or career groups for LGBT+ people who share the same religion, background, or culture.

This may help to show them that these traits and an LGBT+ identity can exist concurrently. It may be useful to recommend the staff member learn about the changes being made so that they see that the medical facility or medical group is promoting inclusion and acceptance, just the way the medical professional promotes this for people of all religions, backgrounds, and cultures.

Often, employees who speak openly in opposition are either repeating what they hear at home or via the media or are trying to sound tough in front of their peers. If an employee speaks up in defiance of LGBT+ inclusive learning material, the change of someone's pronouns, or in any other way, handles the situation publicly and privately. Publicly, address the employee in the moment of their behavior, just as you would for any other insubordination. Depending on what occurs and the commonality of the employee's behavior, this may be a verbal reprimand or refocusing, it may be to remove them from the meeting, or it may be to acknowledge that there will be a formal document in their employee file. This allows all employees to see that you will never tolerate this behavior.

It must also be considered that the employee may be struggling with their own identity or parroting what they hear elsewhere, so it is also important to give the employee the opportunity to explain themselves privately. Ask the employee to talk with you or Human Resources (or both!) and then ask them to explain their comment or action. Their response may warrant a referral to a person who has more power to require a plan or training. They may also simply need guidance that these comments do not impress you or their colleagues and that the repercussions will become increasingly severe if the behavior does not stop. The goal is to provide a strong statement to stop the problem and to provide empathy to avoid escalating the situation.

If the staff member refuses to comply or if you find they have begun to undermine the medical facility's commitment to becoming more LGBT+ inclusive, it is important to document the situation and to bring it to the attention of their supervisor. It does not benefit anyone when an employee is working against the collective goal and it can be detrimental to the mental health and to the physical safety of LGBT+ employees and patients and thus cannot be tolerated. If the staff member is open to learning, shadowing a senior or leadership employee may be beneficial as part of a training or probationary process. If they are not interested in this or if this is not guiding them to become more onboard with the changes to promote LGBT+ inclusion, they may be a better fit for a role that does not interact with other employees or perhaps they would be happier working elsewhere.

Employees' Families (Including Parents, Children, and Other Loved Ones)

Since most employees share their lives with loved ones, the opinions of those outside of your workplace can impact how your employee feels about inclusive changes within the workplace. Many families have limited information regarding LGBT+

people. Their knowledge base may come from the myths and stereotypes they have heard in their own upbringing or from whatever media or news they choose to watch. This can result in substantial fears. While it can be easy for folks to assume that the negative response comes from someone who is stupid or horrible, the reality is that most families are simply trying to advocate for the safety and success of their own employees. Begin by responding to the opposition by assuming good intentions. Offer information about the reason why you are making the choices that they are fighting against.

This may occur by providing statistics of LGBT+ adults suicidality and discussing the medical community's efforts to combat all suicidality by offering the inclusion of various minority groups and via anti-bullying policies. This may come from providing information that talking about sexuality and gender does not actually make a staff member become gay or transgender. It may be necessary to confront the idea that a staff member interacting with an LGBT+ person is not suddenly going to become infected with HIV/AIDS. So often, people's misunderstandings lead them to a place of fear. By calmly providing information and guidance in a way that is not demeaning, you may end the opposition simply through offering the science and research both to end the misunderstanding and by showing how many different marginalized groups are discussed and honored throughout a medical facility.

If this does not work, it is incumbent on the leadership to work with their supervisor to handle the matter just as is done every time an employee complains about something that will not be changed due to that employee's complaint. While so many families want to have control over what and how their employee learns, medical facilities frequently have to let folks know that their feedback is heard but not going to change how things are done. Whatever tactics are used in all other situations of such requests or demands, they can work here too.

Appendix II: Suggested Readings & Resources

(Thank you to the Stanford University—Stanford Medicine, University of Pennsylvania—Penn Medicine, American Medical Association, Human Rights Campaign, PFLAG, American College of Healthcare Executives, Health Professionals Advancing LGBTQ Equality, Center for Disease Control, Health Sherpa, New York Public Library, Loyola University Chicago, The Library of the School of Education at University of Wisconsin–Madison, and the Rainbow Book List for their contributions to this compilation.)

Archives and Collections

James C. Hormel Gay and Lesbian Center

> https://sfpl.org/locations/main-library/lgbtqia-center
> This research center is focused on documenting gay and lesbian history and culture through preservation of original materials and by making them accessible to all. The center is a part of the San Francisco Public Library.

Kinsey Institute at Indiana University—Research, Publications, and Collections

> https://kinseyinstitute.org/collections/index.php
> The Kinsey Institute Collections encompass print materials, film and video, fine art, artifacts, photography, and archives. The Institute has collected publications, objects, art, and data from six continents. Its holding spans more than 2000 years of human history and runs the gamut of technologies—from ink on paper, to microforms and CD-ROMs.

Lesbian Herstory Archives

http://www.lesbianherstoryarchives.org
Located in New York City, the United States, and founded in 1973, this is the
oldest and largest collection of lesbian archives.

Arts, Literature, and Culture

*GLBTQ: An Encyclopedia of Gay, Lesbian. Bisexual, Transgender, and Queer
Culture*

http://www.glbtqarchive.com/
This searchable encyclopedia includes content, bibliographies, and additional
resource links for all things GLBTQ.

Lambada Literary Foundation

http://www.panhandle-florida.com/lambdalitorg/
This organization supports and disseminates works written by and for LGBT+
people.

Here TV

https://www.here.tv/
This site offers a searchable list of queer films.

Queer|Art

https://www.queer-art.org/
Launched in 2009 to support a generation of LGBTQ+ artists that lost mentors to the AIDS Crisis of the 1980s. By fostering the confident expression
of LGBTQ+ artists' perspectives, stories, and identities, Queer|Art amplifies
the voice of a population that has been historically suppressed, disenfran-
chised, and often overlooked by traditional institutional and economic support systems.

Russian Gay Culture

http://community.middlebury.edu/~moss/RGC.html
This site offers literature, films, and history all tied to LGBT people in Russia.

Lesbian and Gay Pulp Fiction Collection at Duke University

https://guides.library.duke.edu/c.php?g=289807&p=1931337
Rubenstein Library's lesbian and gay pulp fiction collections.

E-Journals and Online Newspapers

Advocate

https://www.advocate.com/
The Advocate is a national LGBT magazine and website. They focus on news, politics, opinion, and arts and entertainment for the LGBT community. The Advocate is the oldest and largest LGBT publication in the United States and the only surviving one of its kind that was founded before the 1969 Stonewall Riots in New York City, an incident that is generally credited as the beginning of the LGBT rights movement.

Blithe House Quarterly

www.blithe.com
A collection of gay short fiction is easy to browse on this site.

GLQ: Journal of Lesbian and Gay Studies

http://muse.jhu.edu/journals/glq/index.html
This peer-reviewed journal focuses on the LGBT+ perspective.

National Journal of Sexual Orientation Law

www.ibiblio.org/gaylaw
LGBT legal issues from 1998 to present.

General Information about LGBT+ People and Issues

ACT UP

https://www.actupny.org
This nonpartisan organization aims to end HIV/AIDS stigma and the HIV/AIDS crisis.

Bisexual Resource Center

https://www.biresource.org
This is a resource focused on the bisexual experience and the history of bisexuality via essays and books, plus audio, and visual recordings.

Frameline

https://www.frameline.org
This organization promotes LGBT+ visibility in the media arts field and hosts the oldest and largest media arts event, called the San Francisco International LGBT Film Festival.

Gay and Lesbian Alliance Against Defamation

https://www.glaad.org
Now called GLAAD, this is one of the most well-known organizations intended to promote LGBT+ inclusive representation in the media as a way to combat stereotypes and bigotry.

Gay and Lesbian National Hotline

https://www.glnh.org
This nonprofit offers free anonymous information, referrals, and peer-to-peer counseling.

Gay, Lesbian, and Straight Education Network

www.glsen.org
GLSEN is a leader in the fight against LGBT+ bias in K–12 schools.

Gay Straight Alliance Network (GSA)

https://gsanetwork.org/
GSA Network is a next-generation LGBT+ racial and gender justice organization that empowers queer, trans, and allied youth leaders to advocate, organize, and mobilize an intersectional movement for safer schools and healthier communities.
Check out their Sexual Health Information here: https://gsanetwork.org/sexualhealth

Human Rights Campaign (HRC)

https://www.hrc.org

The HRC represents more than 3 million members and supporters nationwide. As the largest national lesbian, gay, bisexual, transgender, and queer civil rights organization, HRC envisions a world where LGBT+ people are ensured of their basic equal rights and can be open, honest, and safe at home, at work, and in the community.

National Black Justice Coalition

https://www.nbjc.org/
The NBJC is a civil rights organization dedicated to empowering Black lesbian, gay, bisexual, transgender, queer, and same gender loving (LGBT+/SGL) communities, including those living with HIV/AIDS.

National Center for Transgender Equality

https://www.transequality.org/
The National Center for Transgender Equality advocates to change policies and society to increase understanding and acceptance of transgender people. In the nation's capital and throughout the country, NCTE works to replace disrespect, discrimination, and violence with empathy, opportunity, and justice.

The National LGBT+ Task Force (previously The National Gay & Lesbian Task Force)

https://www.thetaskforce.org/
The National LGBT+ Task Force advances full freedom, justice, and equality for LGBT+ people. They are building a future where everyone can be free to be their entire selves in every aspect of their lives. Today, despite all the progress made to end discrimination, millions of LGBT+ people face barriers in every aspect of their lives: in housing, employment, health care, retirement, and basic human rights. These barriers must go. That's why the Task Force is training and mobilizing millions of activists across the nation to deliver a world where you can be you.

Parents, Families & Friends of Lesbians and Gays (PFLAG)

https://www.pflag.org/
Founded in 1973, PFLAG is the first and largest organization dedicated to supporting, educating, and advocating for LGBT++ people and their families. PFLAG's network of hundreds of chapters and more than 325,000 members and supporters works to create a caring, just, and affirming world for LGBT+ people and those who love them.

SAGE

https://www.sageusa.org/
SAGE is the world's oldest and largest nonprofit agency dedicated to serving lesbian, gay, bisexual, and transgender elder communities. They have pioneered programs and services including technical assistance and training to expand opportunities for the aging LGBT community.

The Tegan and Sara Foundation

https://www.teganandsarafoundation.org/
The Tegan and Sara Foundation fights for health, economic justice, and representation for LGBT+ girls and women.

The Trevor Project

https://www.thetrevorproject.org/get-help-now/#sm.0009al7cf1dfiem1vac21yk3 5fehj
The Trevor Project is the leading national organization providing crisis intervention and suicide prevention services to lesbian, gay, bisexual, transgender, and queer youth. Crisis intervention and suicide prevention lifeline: +1-866-488-7386.

History

gayhistory.com

www.gayhistory.com
This website offers an introduction to gay history from 1700 to 1973. It is an ongoing project that consistently adds new materials.

GLBT Historical Society

www.glbthistory.org
This organization collects, preserves, and provides public access to the history of LGBT+ people as individuals and as a community.

Homosexuality in Early Modern Europe

www.uwm.edu/People/jmerrick/hbib.htm
This is a bibliography on homosexuality in Early Modern Europe, which is organized both by country and by subject matter.

Isle of Lesbos

www.sappho.com/about.html
This is a women-oriented gathering of historical documentation of the lives and
views of women both in general and romantically.

Nazi Persecution of Homosexuals, 1933–1945

www.lgbtbarny.org
From the United States Holocaust Memorial Museum, this online exhibit
focuses on the experiences of gay people during World War II.

People with a History

www.fordham.edu/halsall/pwh
Offering historical documentation of LGBT+ people, this site offers an international look at LGBT+ history throughout the world and throughout time.

Law

Lambda Legal Defense and Education Fund

www.lambdalegal.org
This American organization specializes in celebrating and honoring LGBT+
people and people with HIV/AIDS through education, litigation, and public
policy work.

Lesbian/Gay Law Notes

www.lgbtbarny.org
This journal provides information about ongoing court cases, legislations, and
rulings related to LGBT+ people.

Transgender Law Center

https://transgenderlawcenter.org/
Transgender Law Center (TLC) is the largest national trans-led organization
advocating for a world in which all people are free to define themselves and
their futures. Grounded in legal expertise and committed to racial justice,
TLC employs a variety of community-driven strategies to keep transgender
and gender-nonconforming people alive, thriving, and fighting for liberation.

Religion

Affirmation: Gay and Lesbian Mormons

> www.affirmation.org
> This group has chapters around the world to support LGBT+ LDS members and their loved ones by way of socialization and education.

Dignity/USA

> http://dignityusa.org
> This is the largest and most progressive organization for LGBT+ Catholics.

National, Regional, and Local LGBT+ Health Initiatives and Organizations

American Medical Association (AMA)

> www.ama-assn.org/
> Founded in 1847, the AMA is the largest and only national association that convenes 190+ state and specialty medical societies and other critical stakeholders. Throughout history, the AMA has always followed its mission: to promote the art and science of medicine and the betterment of public health.

American Medical Association Advisory Committee on LGBTQ Issues

> https://www.ama-assn.org/member-groups-sections/advisory-committee-lgbtq-issues
> The Advisory Committee on LGBTQ Issues highlights LGBTQ news and topics related to patients and physicians.

AIDS.gov blog

> https://blog.aids.gov/
> Here you will find current blog posts on HIV/AIDS, federal resources, news, guest feature reports, and events.

Center of Excellence for Transgender Health

> http://www.transhealth.ucsf.edu/
> The Center of Excellence for Transgender Health aims to increase access to comprehensive, effective, and affirming health-care services for transgender and gender-variant communities.

Center for American Progress (LGBT)

https://www.americanprogress.org/issues/lgbt/view/
CAP is a think tank dedicated to improving the lives of Americans through ideas and action, combining bold policy ideas with a modern communications platform to help shape the national debate. CAP is designed to provide long-term leadership and support to the progressive movement. CAP's policy experts on LGBT Research and Communications have a dedicated area on its website with evidence-based reports.

Centers for Disease Control (CDC) LGBT Health Homepage

www.cdc.gov/lgbthealth/
CSC's website from the U.S. government on covering information on LGBT health topics.

Center for LGBT Health Research at University of Pittsburgh

https://pre.lgbthlres.pitt.edu/
The mission of the Center is to understand and improve the health of the LGBT community by maintaining an infrastructure that provides research concerning LGBT health and wellness needs.

The Child and Adolescent Gender Center

https://diversitybch.ucsf.edu/child-and-adolescent-gender-center
A collaboration between UCSF and community organizations that offers comprehensive medical and psychological care, as well as advocacy and legal support, to gender nonconforming/transgender youth and adolescents.

The Fenway Institute

https://www.thefenwayinstitute.org
Fenway's mission is to enhance the well-being of the LGBT+ community and all people in its neighborhoods and beyond through access to the highest quality health care, education, research and advocacy.

Gay Men's Health Crisis (GMHC)

www.gmhc.org/
The organization's focus on services for people living with AIDS continues and includes HIV education, prevention, care, and advocacy.

Gay Parents to Be

https://www.gayparentstobe.com/
Gay Parents To Be provides care for LGBT+ couples and individuals as they consider their options around building a family.

GLMA: Health Professionals Advancing LGBTQ Equality (previously the Gay & Lesbian Medical Association)

https://www.glma.org/
GLMA represents both the interests of LGBT+ health professionals of all kinds, as well as millions of LGBT+ patients and families. It addresses the full spectrum of LGBT+ health topics, including breast and cervical cancer, hepatitis, mental health, HIV/AIDS, substance use, tobacco use, access to care for transgender persons, and behavioral health.

Gay, Lesbian and Straight Education Network

https://www.glsen.org
GLSEN is a leader in the fight against LGBT+ bias in K–12 schools.

Gender Spectrum

https://www.genderspectrum.org/
A national organization committed to the health and well-being of gender-diverse children and teens through education and support for families, and training and guidance for educators, medical and mental health providers, and other professionals.

The Goldsen Institute at the University of Washington

https://goldseninstitute.org/
Conducts Innovative Research in Health, Longevity, Sexuality, Gender and Culture.

Healthy People 2030

https://health.gov/healthypeople/objectives-and-data/browse-objectives/lgbt
Produced by the Office of Disease Prevention and Health Promotion (ODPHP), this is the key science-based, 10-year national objectives for improving the health of all Americans which historically includes Lesbian, Gay, Bisexual and Transgender Health. LGBT+ health experts produced an LGBT compendium document to Healthy People 2010.

HIV Prevention Justice Alliance

https://www.preventionjustice.org/
The HIV Prevention Justice Alliance focuses on HIV/AIDS by sharing information, collaborating on strategic campaigns, and taking bold action to win lifesaving policy changes.

Howard Brown Health Center

https://howardbrown.org/
Howard Brown Health exists to eliminate the disparities in health-care experienced by lesbian, gay, bisexual, and transgender people through research, education, and the provision of services that promote health and wellness.

Kinsey Institute at Indiana University

https://kinseyinstitute.org/
For over 75 years, the Kinsey Institute at Indiana University has been the trusted source for scientific knowledge and research on critical issues in sexuality, gender, and reproduction.

LGBTData.com from Drexel University

http://www.lgbtdata.com/
LGBTData.com serves as a no-cost, open-access clearinghouse for the collection of sexual orientation and gender identity data and measures.

LGBT Health Journal

http://www.liebertpub.com/lgbt
Published six times per year, this journal profiles new and cutting-edge science-based LGBT+ health research articles on current and emerging issues.

LGBT Health Link Network

https://www.lgbthealthlink.org/
A website that offers exclusive content and resources to those working to enhance LGBT health by reducing health disparities within our communities.

LGBTQIA+ Health Education Center

https://www.lgbtqiahealtheducation.org/

The National LGBTQIA+ Health Education Center aims to advance health equity for LGBTQIA+ people and the populations which may intersect with the LGBTQIA+ community, address, and eliminate health disparities for the LGBTQIA+ community, optimize access to cost-effective health care for the LGBTQIA+ community, and improve the quality of care for LGBTQIA+ people by providing training and technical assistance to health-care providers and staff across the globe.

National Association of Lesbian and Gay Addiction Professionals

https://www.nalgap.org/
NALGAP: The Association of Lesbian, Gay, Bisexual, Transgender Addiction Professionals and Their Allies is a membership organization founded in 1979 and dedicated to the prevention and treatment of alcoholism, substance use, and other addictions in lesbian, gay, bisexual, transgender, and queer communities.

The National Coalition for *LGBT Health*

https://www.healthhiv.org/sites-causes/national-coalition-for-lgbt-health/
The National Coalition for LGBT Health project seeks to de-stigmatize LGBTQ health care and raise awareness of LGBTQ health disparities. The coalition also seeks to expand cultural competency for the diverse LGBTQ population, and to improve both access to, and utilization of, health-care resources.

National Healthcare Equality Index (HEI)—HRC's annual hospital survey

https://www.hrc.org/HEI
A national LGBTQ benchmarking tool that evaluates health-care facilities' policies and practices.

National HIV/AIDS Strategy (NHAS)

https://files.hiv.gov/s3fs-public/2022-09/NHAS_Federal_Implementation_Plan.pdf
Launched in 2009, The White House issued the NHAS for the United States to reflect many of the approaches the CDC believes will reduce HIV incidence.

National LGBT Cancer Network

https://cancer-network.org/
The National LGBT Cancer Network works to improve the lives of LGBT cancer survivors and those at risk by education the LGBT community about the increased cancer risks and the importance of screening and early detection; training health-care providers to offer more culturally competent, safe, and

welcoming care; and advocating for LGBT survivors in mainstream cancer organizations, the media, and research.

The National LGBT Cancer Project

https://www.lgbtcancer.org/
The National LGBT Cancer Project is the United States' first and leading Lesbian, Gay, Bisexual and Transgendered cancer survivor support and advocacy nonprofit organization, committed to improving the health of LGBT cancer survivors with peer-to-peer support.

National Resource Center on LGBT Aging

https://www.lgbtagingcenter.org/
The National Resource Center on LGBTQ+ Aging is the country's first and only technical assistance resource center focused on improving the quality of services and supports offered to lesbian, gay, bisexual, and/or transgender older adults, their families, and caregivers.

OutCare

https://www.outcarehealth.org/
OutCare Health is a nonprofit 501(c)(3) organization with the purpose of providing extensive information and education on lesbian, gay, bisexual, transgender, and queer (LGBTQ) health care.

Out2Enroll

https://out2enroll.org/
Out2Enroll is a national organization focused on connecting the LGBTQ community with health insurance resources and ACA enrollment support.

QSPACES

https://www.qspaces.org/
QSPACES is building a free website for LGBTQ folks to find, rate, and review health and wellness providers on LGBTQ-friendliness, competency, and overall care.

Queer Health Access

https://www.queerhealthaccess.com/
The Queer Health Access consolidates the various resources in the marketplace centered for LGBTQ Women and Girls.

Resource Center for Minority Data from ICPSR at the University of Michigan

> https://www.icpsr.umich.edu/web/pages/RCMD/index.html
> The mission for the Resource Center for Minority Data (RCMD) is to provide educators, researchers, and students with data resources so that they can produce analysis of issues affecting minority populations in the United States.

Substance Abuse and Mental Health Service Administration (SAMHSA)

> https://www.samhsa.gov/behavioral-health-equity/lgbtqi
> Resources on the LGBTQI+ population include national survey reports, agency and federal initiatives, and related behavioral health resources.

Straight for Equality in Healthcare (PFLAG)

> https://www.straightforequality.org/healthcare
> Straight for Equality in Healthcare invites health-care providers to join to find out more about what it means to be an ally in health care, learn more about the specific health-care concerns/needs of the lesbian, gay, bisexual, transgender, and queer (LGBTQ+) community, and/or look for everyday actions they can take to support LGBTQ+ people at their practice.

Trans-Health.com

> https://www.trans-health.com/
> Find timely information for medical professionals and transgender/gender-expansive people alike. The site discusses policy changes, advocacy work, and guidelines for working with transgender and gender-expansive individuals.

UCSF, Division of Prevention Science

> https://prevention.ucsf.edu/
> The University of California San Francisco's Division of Prevention Science is home to the Center for AIDS Prevention Studies, the Center of Excellence for Transgender Health, the UCSF Prevention Research Center, and the Health Equity Action Network.

The World Professional Association for Transgender Health, Inc. (WPATH)

> https://www.wpath.org/
> Founded as the Harry Benjamin International Gender Dysphoria Association (HBIGDA) in 1979, the World Professional Association for Transgender

Health (WPATH) is a 501(c)(3) interdisciplinary professional and educational organization devoted to transgender health. Its stated mission is to promote evidence-based care, education, research, advocacy, public policy, and respect in transgender health. To support that mission, the organization engages in clinical and academic research to improve the quality of care provided to transsexual, transgender, and gender-expansive individuals globally.

Select LGBT+ Health Publications

The Joint Commission's Advancing Effective Communication, Cultural Competence, and Patient- and Family-Centered Care for the Lesbian, Gay, Bisexual and Transgender (LGBT) Community: A Field Guide

https://www.jointcommission.org/lgbt/

The American Health Layers Association's *Revisiting Your Hospital's Visitation Policy*

https://www.healthlawyers.org/hlresources/PI/InfoSeries/Pages/RevisitingYour Hospital'sVisitationPolicy.aspx

CAP Report on LGBT Health Disparities

https://www.americanprogress.org/issues/2009/12/lgbt_health_disparities.html

Columbia University—GLMA White Paper—LGBT Health: Findings and Concerns

www.glma.org/_data/n_0001/resources/live/ColumbiaWhitePaper2.pdf

Department of Health & Human Services LGBT health webpages

https://www.hhs.gov/secretary/about/lgbthealth.html

Family Acceptance Project (San Francisco State University)

familyproject.sfsu.edu/publications
These findings are used in a wide variety of ways to help families, providers, clergy, youth, and policymakers to decrease risk and promote well-being for LGBTQ children and youth and to strengthen families.

The Fenway Institute's Improving the Health Care of Lesbian, Gay, Bisexual and Transgender (LGBT) People: Understanding and Eliminating Health Disparities

> https://fenwayhealth.org/fenway-health-clinicians-and-researchers-author-first-edition-of-transgender-and-gender-diverse-health-care-the-fenway-guide-published-by-mcgraw-hill-professional/

GLMA's Clinical Guidelines for Care of LGBT Patients

> https://www.glma.org/_data/n_0001/resources/live/WelcomingEnvironment.pdf

The Goldsen Institute at University of Washington's The Aging & Health Report: Disparities and Resilience among LGBT Older Adults.

> https://goldseninstitute.org/allresources/

Institute of Medicine's The Health of Lesbian, Gay, Bisexual, and Transgender People: Building a Foundation for Better Understanding

> https://www.nap.edu/catalog/13128/the-health-of-lesbian-gay-bisexual-and-transgender-people-building

Kaiser Permanente Provider's Handbook on Culturally Competent Care: LGBT Population

> https://www.madisonstreetpress.com/cgi-bin/shop.shtml?id=25

Kinsey Institute at Indiana University—Research and Publications

> Research and publications that cover topics such as condom use, effects of trauma, relationships' dynamic and social life study, and more. https://kinseyinstitute.org/research/index.php

Lambda Legal's *When Health Care Isn't Caring*

> https://www.lambdalegal.org/publications/when-health-care-isnt-caring

LGBTQ Cultures: What Health Care Professionals Need to Know About Sexual & Gender Diversity, Michele J. Eliason et al.

> https://www.nursingcenter.com/upload/journals/documents/9781496343130.html

Substance Abuse and Mental Health Services Administration's *Top Health Issues for LGBT Populations: Information Resources Kit*

> http://store.samhsa.gov/product/Top-Health-Issues-for-LGBT-Populations/ SMA12-4684

LGBT-Related Medical Education Resources

American Medical Student Association (AMSA)

> www.amsa.org/
> We're the American Medical Student Association—we exist to prepare, train, and embolden medical students to become leaders. Advocates for quality and affordable health care for all. Ushers of a better, more inclusive, equitable future. With over 30,000 members from across the globe, AMSA is the largest and oldest independent association of physicians-in-training in the United States.

Association of American Medical Colleges (AAMC)

> www.aamc.org/
> The AAMC leads and serves the academic medicine community to improve the health of people everywhere. Founded in 1876 and based in Washington, DC, the AAMC is a not-for-profit association dedicated to transforming health through medical education, health care, medical research, and community collaborations.

Consortium of Higher Education Lesbian Gay Bisexual Transgender Resource Professionals

> https://www.lgbtcampus.org/
> Support individuals who work on campuses to educate and support people of diverse sexual orientations and gender identities, as well as advocate for more inclusive policies and practices through an intersectional and racial justice framework.

Provider-Specific Resources

American Cancer Society—brochures on LGBT cancer and smoking

> https://www.cancer.org or contact local ACS office

American Medical Association—How to create an LGBTQ friendly practice

> https://www.ama-assn.org/delivering-care/population-care/creating-lgbtq-friendly-practice

Family Acceptance Project—A Practitioner's Resource Guide: Helping Families to Support Their LGBT Children

> https://store.samhsa.gov/system/files/pep14-lgbtkids.pdf

Gay, Lesbian, Bisexual, and Transgender (GLBT) Health Access Project—posters and protocols

> https://www.glbthealth.org

GLMA: Health Professionals Advancing LGBTQ Equality—Many Resources for Medical Professionals

> Guidelines for the care of LGBT patients
> https://www.glma.org/_data/n_0001/resources/live/GLMA%20guidelines%20
> 2006%20FINAL.pdf
> Same-Sex Marriage and Health
> https://www.glma.org/index.cfm?fuseaction=Page.ViewPage&PageID=850
> Additional Resources include Provider Directory, Provider Guidelines for
> Creating a Welcoming Environments, Reports, Research, and more.
> https://www.glma.org/index.cfm?fuseaction=Page.viewPage&pageId=940&par
> entID=534
> Webinar: Quality Health Care for Lesbian, Gay, Bisexual & Transgender
> People: A series of YouTube webinars on understanding the health needs of
> LGBT patients.
> https://www.youtube.com/watch?v=8mQOGtVUoaM

Human Rights Campaign—LGBTQ+ Youth Resources

> https://www.hrc.org/youth#.T9USGXG82EA

Lambda Legal—Creating Equal Access to Quality Healthcare for Transgender Patients

> https://www.lambdalegal.org/publications/fs_transgender-affirming-
> hospital-policies

National Coalition for LGBT Health (Center for American Progress)—Changing the Game: What Health Care Reform Means for GLBT Americans

> www.americanprogress.org/issues/2011/03/pdf/aca_lgbt.pdf

National LGBTQIA+ Health Education Center—Various Resources from webinars to guides

https://www.lgbtqiahealtheducation.org/resources/

National Resource Center on LGBT Aging—Inclusive Services for LGBT Older Adults—A Practical Guide for Creating Welcoming Agencies

https://www.pennmedicine.org/-/media/documents%20and%20audio/patient%20guides%20and%20instructions/lgbt%20health/national_resource_center_lgbt_aging_2016.ashx?la=en

U.S. Department of Health and Human Services: Recommended actions to improve the health and well-being of lesbian, gay, bisexual, and transgender communities.

https://www.hhs.gov/programs/topic-sites/lgbt/index.html
https://www.hhs.gov/secretary/about/lgbthealth.html

Transgender Law Center

Tips for welcoming transgender patients
https://www.transgenderlawcenter.org

The University of California, San Francisco's Center of Excellence for Transgender Health—primary care protocols

https://transhealth.ucsf.edu/

Resources for LGBT+ People and Their Families

Family Acceptance Project—Resources for families of LGBT youth

http://familyproject.sfsu.edu/

Family Equality Council—Resources for LGBT families

https://www.familyequality.org

GLMA: Health Professionals Advancing LGBTQ Equality—Many Resources for Patients

https://www.glma.org/index.cfm?fuseaction=Page.viewPage&pageId=939&grandparentID=534&parentID=938&nodeID=1

Resources include Find a Provider, Healthcare Equality Index, 10 Things Gay Men Should Discuss with Their Healthcare Providers, 10 Things Lesbians Should Discuss with Their Healthcare Providers, 10 Things Bisexuals Should Discuss with Their Healthcare Providers, and 10 Things Transgender Persons Should Discuss with Their Healthcare Providers.

Human Rights Campaign Foundation—LGBTQ Patient Resources

https://www.hrc.org/resources/patient-resources

Lambda Legal—Tools for Protecting Your Health Care Wishers

glma.org/_data/n_0001/resources/live/ttp_your-health-care-wishes.pdf

UCSF—Eight Best Practices for HIV Prevention among Trans People

transhealth.ucsf.edu/pdf/bp-prevention.pdf

Appendix III: Suggested Reading for Youth

The following list includes age recommendations but remember to consider the reading levels and abilities of your students rather than to rely on age recommendations when choosing which to recommend or include in your waiting rooms and tools to use with youth. Please note that books should be reviewed by you or a trusted person for any potential triggers before being recommended to youth and that there may be safety risks in recommending these to youth who may not be out at home.

General Books about LGBT+ Issues: Nonfiction

Alsenas, Linas. Gay America: Struggle for Equality. Amulet, 2008. 160 pages. Age 12 and older

Bausum, Ann. Stonewall: Breaking Out in the Fight for Gay Rights. Viking, 2015. 120 pages. Age 13 and older

Krakow, Kari. The Harvey Milk Story. Illustrated by David Gardner. Two Lives Publishing, 2002. 32 pages. Ages 6–10

Levithan, David and Billy Merrill, editors. Full Spectrum: A New Generation of Writing About Gay, Lesbian, Bisexual, Transgender, Questioning, and Other Identities. Alfred A. Knopf, 2006. 272 pages. Ages 13 and older

Marcus, Eric. What If Someone I Know Is Gay? Answers to Questions about What It Means to be Gay or Lesbian. Simon Pulse, 2007. 183 pages. Ages 12 and older

Winick, Judd. Pedro and Me: Friendship. Loss, and What I Learned. Henry Holt, 2000. 187 pages. Ages 12–18

General Books about LGBT+ Issues: Fiction

Brothers, Meagan. <u>Debbie Harry Sings in French</u>. Henry Holt, 2008. 240 pages. Ages 13 and up

Trueman, Terry. <u>7 Days at the Hot Corner</u>. HarperTempest/Harper Collins, 2007. 150 pages. Ages 12 and older

Families with Gay and Lesbian Parents or Other Adult Relatives: Nonfiction

Combs, Bobbie. <u>1, 2, 3: A Family Counting Book</u>. Illustrated by Danamarie Hosler. Two Lives, 2001. 29 pages. Ages 2–5

Combs, Bobbie. <u>ABC: A Family Alphabet Book</u>. Illustrated by Desiree Keane and Brian Rappa. Two Lives, 2001. 32 pages. Ages 2–5

Jenness, Aylette. <u>Families: A Celebration of Diversity, Commitment, and Love</u>. Houghton Mifflin, 1990. 48 pages. Ages 5–12

Kuklin, Susan. <u>Families</u>. Hyperion, 2005. 36 pages. Ages 7–11

Families with Gay and Lesbian Parents or Other Adult Relatives: Picture Books

Brannen, Sarah S. <u>Uncle Bobby's Wedding</u>. Putnam, 2008. 32 pages. Ages 5–8

Caines, Jeannette. <u>Just Us Women</u>. Illustrated by Pat Cummings. Harper, 1982. 32 pages. Ages 4–6

De Veaux, Alexiz. <u>An Enchanted Hair Tale</u>. Illustrated by Cheryl Hanna. Harper & Row, 1987. 40 pages. Ages 5–10

DeHaan, Linda. <u>King & King</u>. Illustrated by Stern Nijland. Tricycle Press, 2002. 32 pages. Ages 5–7

DeHaan, Linda. <u>King & King & Family</u>. Illustrated by Stern Nijland. Tricycle Press, 2004. 32 pages. Ages 5–8

Fogliano, Julie. <u>Old Dog Baby</u>. Illustrated by Chris Raschka. A Neal Porter Book/Roaring Brook Press, 2016. 32 pages. Ages 2–4

Garden, Nancy. <u>Molly's Family</u>. Illustrated by Sharon Wooding. Farrar Straus Giroux, 2004. 32 pages. Ages 5–8

Lambert, Megan Dowd. <u>Real Sisters Pretend</u>. Illustrated by Nicole Tadgell. Tilbury House, 2016. 32 pages. Ages 4–7

Levine, Arthur A. <u>Monday Is One Day</u>. Illustrated by Julian Hector. Scholastic Press, 2011. 28 pages. Ages 2–4

Lindenbaum, Pija. <u>Mini Mia and Her Darling Uncle</u>. Translated by Elisabeth Kallick Dyssegaard. U.S. edition: R&S Books, 2007. 40 pages. Ages 3–6

Newman, Lesléa. <u>Daddy, Papa, and Me</u>. Illustrated by Carol Thompson. Tricycle Press, 2009. 16 pages. Ages birth–3

Newman, Lesléa. <u>Mommy, Mama, and Me</u>. Illustrated by Carol Thompson. Tricycle Press, 2009. 16 pages. Ages birth–3

Newman, Lesléa. <u>Heather Has Two Mommies (new edition)</u>. Illustrated by Laura Cornell. Candlewick Press, 2015. 32 pages. Ages 3–6

Oelschlager, Vanita. <u>A Tale of Two Daddies</u>. Illustrated by Kristin Blackwood and Mike Blanc. Vanita Books, 2010. 40 pages. Ages 3–8

Polacco, Patricia. <u>In Our Mothers' House</u>. Philomel, 2009. 48 pages. Ages 6–10

Richardson, Justin and Peter Parnell. <u>And Tango Makes Three</u>. Illustrated by Henry Cole. Simon & Schuster, 2005. 32 pages. Ages 3–6

Sima, Jessie. <u>Harriet Gets Carried Away</u>. Simon & Schuster, 2018. 42 pages. Ages 3–6

Warhola, James. <u>Uncle Andy's: A Faabbbulous Visit with Andy Warhol</u>. Putnam, 2003. 32 pages. Ages 6–10

Williams, Vera B. <u>Three Days on a River in a Red Canoe</u>. Greenwillow, 1981. 32 pages. Ages 4–9

Williams, Vera B. <u>Home at Last</u>. Illustrated by Vera B. Williams and Chris Raschka. Greenwillow/HarperCollins, 2016. Ages 6–10

Families with Gay and Lesbian Parents or Other Adult Relatives: Fiction

Freymann-Weyr, Garret. <u>My Heartbeat</u>. Houghton Mifflin, 2002. 154 pages. Ages 13 and up

Ignatow, Amy. <u>The Popularity Papers: Research for the Social Improvement and General Betterment of Lydia Goldblatt & Julie Graham-Chang</u>. Abrams, 2010. 204 pages. Ages 8–11

Levy, Dana Alison. <u>The Misadventures of the Family Fletcher</u>. Delacorte, 2014. 260 pages. Ages 7–10

Levy, Dana Alison. <u>The Family Fletcher Takes Rock Island</u>. Delacorte Press, 2016. 259 pages. Ages 7–10

Peters, Julie Anne. <u>Between Mom and Jo</u>. Little, Brown, 2006. 232 pages. Ages 13 and up

Woodson, Jacqueline. <u>After Tupac and D Foster</u>. Putnam, 2008. 153 pages. Ages 10–14

Woodson, Jacqueline. <u>From the Notebooks of Melanin Sun</u>. Blue Sky/ Scholastic, 1995. 141 pages. Ages 11–15

LGBT+ Children and Teens: Nonfiction

Andrews, Arin and Joshua Lyon. <u>Some Assembly Required: The Not-So-Secret Life of a Transgender Teen</u>. Simon & Schuster, 2014. 248 pages. Ages 12 and older

Jennings, Jazz. <u>My Life as a (Transgender) Teen</u>. Ember. 2017. 272 pages. Ages 12 and older

Kuklin, Susan. <u>Beyond Magenta: Transgender Teens Speak Out</u>. Candlewick Press, 2014. 182 pages. Age 12 and older

Thrash, Maggie. <u>Honor Girl</u>. Candlewick Press, 2015. 267 pages. Age 13 and older

Walden, Tillie. <u>Spinning</u>. First Second, 2017. 395 pages. Age 13 and older

LGBT+ Children and Teens: Fiction

Bantle, Lee. <u>David Inside Out</u>. Christy Ottaviano Books/Henry Holt, 2009. 184 pages. Ages 15 and older

Beam, Cris. <u>I Am J</u>. Little, Brown, 2011. 326 pages. Age 13 and older

Block, Francesca Lia. <u>Weetzie Bat</u>. Charlotte Zolotow Book/Harper & Row, 1989. 88 pages. Ages 13 and older

Bray, Libba. <u>Beauty Queens</u>. Scholastic Press, 2011. 396 pages. Age 13 and older

Brooks, Kevin. <u>Black Rabbit Summer</u>. U.S. edition: The Chicken House/ Scholastic, 2008. 488 pages. Age 13 and older

Buckell, Tobias S. and Joe Monti, editors. <u>Diverse Energies</u>. Tu Books, 2012. 314 pages. Age 12 and older

Cameron, Peter. <u>Someday This Pain Will Be Useful to You</u>. Frances Foster Books/Farrar, Straus, and Giroux, 2007. 229 pages. Ages 14 and up

Cart, Michael. <u>How Beautiful the Ordinary</u>. HarperTeen/HarperCollins, 2009. 350 pages. Ages 15 and older

Carter, Timothy. <u>Evil?</u> Flux, 2009. 264 pages. Ages 14 and older

Cohn, Rachel and David Levithan. <u>Naomi and Ely's No-Kiss List</u>. Alfred A. Knopf, 2007. 230 pages. Ages 14 and older

Danforth, Emily M. <u>The Miseducation of Cameron Post</u>. Balzer + Bray/HarperCollins, 2012. 470 pages. Age 14 and older

Dee, Barbara. <u>Star-Crossed</u>. Aladdin, 2017. 277 pages. Ages 9–12

Dole, Mayra Lazara. <u>Down to the Bone</u>. HarperTeen/HarperCollins, 2008. 367 pages. Age 14 and older

Downham, Jenny. <u>Unbecoming</u>. David Fickling Books/Scholastic, 2016. 375 pages. Age 14 and older

Farizan, Sara. <u>Tell Me Again How a Crush Should Feel</u>. Algonquin, 2014. 296 pages. Ages 13 and older

Farizan, Sara. <u>If You Could Be Mine</u>. Algonquin, 2013. 248 pages. Age 13 and older

Federle, Tim. <u>Five, Six, Seven, Nate!</u>. Simon & Schuster, 2014. 293 pages. Ages 8–11

Felin, M. Sindy. <u>Touching Snow</u>. Atheneum, 2007. 234 pages. Ages 13 and up

Garden, Nancy. <u>Annie on My Mind</u>. Farrar, Straus, Giroux, 1981. 234 pages. Ages 12–15

Garden, Nancy. <u>Hear Us Out! Lesbian and Gay Stories of Struggle, Progress and Hope, 1950 to the Present</u>. Farrar, Straus, and Giroux, 2007. 227 pages. Age 12 and older

Garvin, Jeff. <u>Symptoms of Being Human</u>. Balzer + Bray/HarperCollins, 2016. 335 pages. Age 14 and older

George, Madeleine. <u>The Difference Between You and Me</u>. Viking, 2012. 256 pages. Age 12 and older

Girard, M.-E. <u>Girl Mans Up</u>. HarperTeen, 2016. 373 pages. Age 14 and older

Goldman, Steven. <u>Two Parties, One Tux, and a Very Short Film about the Grapes of Wrath</u>. Bloomsbury, 2008. 307 pages. Age 14 and older

Goode, Laura. <u>Sister Mischief</u>. Candlewick Press, 2011. 367 pages. Age 14 and older

Green, John and David Levithan. <u>Will Grayson, Will Grayson</u>. Penguin, 2010. 304 pages. Age 14 and older

Griffin, Molly Beth. <u>Silhouette of a Sparrow</u>. Milkweed Editions, 2012. 189 pages. Age 13 and older

Hartinger, Brent. <u>Geography Club</u>. HarperCollins, 2003. 226 pages. Ages 13 and up

Hartinger, Brent. <u>The Order of the Poison Oak</u>. HarperTempest, 2005. 211 pages. Ages 12–18

Hartinger, Brent. <u>Split Screen</u>. HarperTempest/HarperCollins, 2007. 288 pages. Ages 12–16

Hegamin, Tonya Cheri. <u>M+O 4evr</u>. Houghton Mifflin, 2008. 165 pages. Age 14 and older

Howe, James. <u>Totally Joe</u>. Ginee Seo Books/Atheneum, 2005. 189 pages. Ages 10–14

Hurwin, Davida Wills. <u>Freaks and Revelations</u>. Little, Brown, 2009. 234 pages. Ages 14 and older

Hutchinson, Shaun David. <u>We Are the Ants</u>. Simon Pulse, 2016. 451 pages. Age 14 and older

King, A. S. <u>Ask the Passengers</u>. Little, Brown, 2012. 292 pages. Age 13 and older

Kluger, Steve. <u>My Most Excellent Year: A Novel of Love, Mary Poppins, and Fenway Park</u>. Dial, 2008. 416 pages

Knowles, Jo. <u>See You at Harry's</u>. Candlewick Press, 2012. 310 pages. Ages 11–14

Kokie, E. M. <u>Personal Effects</u>. Candlewick Press, 2012. 341 pages. Age 14 and older

Kokie, E. M. <u>Radical</u>. Candlewick Press, 2016. 437 pages. Age 14 and older

Konigsberg, Bill. <u>The Porcupine of Truth</u>. Arthur A. Levine Books/ Scholastic, 2015. 325 pages. Age 14 and older

Konigsberg, Bill. <u>Openly Straight</u>. Arthur A. Levine Books, 2013. 320 pages. Age 14 and older

Konigsberg, Bill. <u>Out of the Pocket</u>. Dutton, 2008. 264 pages. Age 13 and older

LaRochelle, David. <u>Absolutely, Positively, Not …</u>. Arthur A. Levine Books/ Scholastic Press, 2005. 224 pages. Ages 12 and older

Levithan, David. <u>Boy Meets Boy</u>. Alfred A. Knopf, 2003. 185 pages. Ages 12–15

Levithan, David. <u>How They Met and Other Stories</u>. Knopf, 2008. 244 pages. Age 13 and older

Lo, Malindo. <u>Ash</u>. Little, Brown, 2009. 264 pages. Ages 13 and older

Magoon, Kekla. <u>37 Things I Love (in No Particular Order)</u>. Henry Holt, 2012. 224 pages. Age 12 and older

Malloy, Brian. <u>Twelve Long Months</u>. Scholastic, 2007. 320 pages. Ages 14–18

McLemore, Anna-Marie. <u>When the Moon Was Ours</u>. Thomas Dunne Books/St. Martin's Griffin, 2016. 273 pages. Age 14 and older

McLemore, Anna-Marie. <u>Wild Beauty</u>. Feiwel and Friends, 2017. 339 pages. Age 14 and older

Medina, Nico. <u>The Straight Road to Kylie</u>. Simon Pulse, 2007. 320 pages. Ages 14–18

Ness, Patrick. <u>Release</u>. HarperTeen, 2017. 277 pages. Age 15 and older

Newman, Lesléa. <u>October Mourning: A Song for Matthew Shepard</u>. Candlewick Press, 2012. 128 pages. Age 13 and older

Peck, Dale. <u>Sprout</u>. Bloomsbury, 2009. 277 pages. Ages 13 and older

Peters, Julie Ann. <u>Far from Xanadu</u>. Megan Tingley Books/Little, Brown, 2005. 282 pages. Ages 13–17

Peters, Julie Anne. <u>grl2grl: Short Fictions</u>. Megan Tingley Books/Little, Brown, 2007. 151 pages. Ages 14 and up

Peters, Julie Anne. <u>Keeping You a Secret</u>. A Megan Tingley Book/Little, Brown, 2003. 250 pages. Ages 14–16

Peters, Julie Anne. <u>Luna</u>. Megan Tingley Books/Little Brown, 2004. 247 pages. Ages 14–17

Podos, Rebecca. <u>Like Water</u>. Balzer + Bray, 2017. 312 pages. Age 13 and older

Polonsky, Ami. <u>Gracefully Grayson</u>. Disney Hyperion, 2014. 243 pages. Ages 10–13

Rowell, Rainbow. <u>Carry On</u>. St. Martin's Griffin, 2015. 528 pages. Age 12 and older

Ruditis, Paul. <u>The Four Dorothys</u>. Simon Pulse, 2007. 243 pages. Ages 12–16

Ryan, P. E. <u>Saints of Augustine</u>. HarperTeen/HarperCollins, 2007. 308 pages. Ages 14 and up

Sáenz, Benjamin Alire. <u>The Inexplicable Logic of My Life</u>. Clarion/Houghton Mifflin Harcourt, 2017. 464 pages. Age 13 and older

Sáenz, Benjamin Alire. <u>Aristotle and Dante Discover the Secrets of the Universe</u>. Simon & Schuster, 2012. 359 pages. Age 14 and older

Sanchez, Alex. <u>So Hard To Say</u>. Simon & Schuster, 2004. 230 pages. Ages 12–15

Schmatz, Pat. <u>Lizard Radio</u>. Candlewick Press, 2015. 280 pages. Age 13 and older

Silvera, Adam. <u>More Happy Than Not</u>. Soho Teen/Soho Press, 2015. 295 pages. Age 14 and older

Smith, Andrew. <u>Grasshopper Jungle</u>. Dutton, 2014. 388 pages. Age 14 and older

St. James, James. <u>Freak Show</u>. Dutton, 2007. 298 pages. Age 13 and older

Tamaki, Mariko. <u>Skim</u>. Illustrated by Jillian Tamaki. Groundwood Books/House of Anansi Press, 2008. 141 pages. 14 and up

Trueman, Terry. <u>7 Days at the Hot Corner</u>. HarperTempest/HarperCollins, 2007. 150 pages. Ages 12 and older

van Dijk, Lutz. <u>Damned Strong Love: The True Story of Willi G. and Stefan K.: A Novel</u>. Translated by Elizabeth D. Crawford, from the German. U.S. edition: Henry Holt, 1995. 138 pages. Ages 14–18

Whaley, John Corey. <u>Highly Illogical Behavior</u>. Dial, 2016. 249 pages. Age 14 and older

Wilson, Martin. <u>What They Always Tell Us</u>. Delacorte Press, 2008. 293 pages. Age 14 and older

Wittlinger, Ellen. <u>Love & Lies: Marisol's Story</u>. Simon & Schuster, 2008. 256 pages. Age 14 and older

Wittlinger, Ellen. <u>Parrotfish</u>. Simon & Schuster, 2007. 294 pages. Ages 14 and up

Wolff, Virginia Euwer. <u>True Believer</u>. Atheneum, 2001. 264 pages. Ages 13–16

Wyeth, Sharon Dennis. <u>Orphea Proud</u>. Delacorte Press, 2004. 208 pages. Ages 14–17

Sex and Gender Identity/Gender Nonconformity

Baldacchino, Christine. <u>Morris Micklewhite and the Tangerine Dress</u>. Illustrated by Isabelle Malenfant. A Groundwood Book/House of Anansi Press, 2014. 32 pages. Ages 3–8

Cassidy, Sara. <u>A Boy Named Queen</u>. Groundwood, 2016. 77 pages. Ages 7–10

DePaola, Tomie. <u>Oliver Button Is a Sissy</u>. Harcourt, 1979. 48 pages

DiPucchio, Kelly. <u>Gaston</u>. Illustrated by Christian Robinson. Atheneum, 2014. 32 pages. Ages 4–8

Fierstein, Harvey. <u>The Sissy Duckling</u>. Illustrated by Henry Cole. Simon & Schuster, 2002. 40 pages. Ages 5–7

Gino, Alex. <u>George</u>. Scholastic Press, 2015. 240 pages. Ages 8–11

Harris, Robie. <u>It's So Amazing! A Book about Eggs, Sperm, Birth, Babies, and Families</u>. Illustrated by Michael Emberly. Candlewick, 1999. 81 pages. Ages 7–10

Harris, Robie. <u>It's Perfectly Normal: Changing Bodies, Growing Up, Sex & Sexual Health</u>. Illustrated by Michael Emberley. Candlewick, 1994. 89 pages. Ages 9–12

Hashimi, Nadia. <u>One Half from the East</u>. HarperCollins, 2016. 272 pages. Ages 9–13

Herthel, Jessica and Jazz Jennings. <u>I Am Jazz</u>. Illustrated by Shelagh McNicholas. Dial, 2014. 24 pages. Ages 3–9

Hoffman, Sarah and Ian Hoffman. <u>Jacob's New Dress</u>. Illustrated by Chris Case. Albert Whitman, 2014. 32 pages. Ages 3–8

Huser, Glen. <u>Stitches</u>. Groundwood/Douglas & McIntyre, 2003. 198 pages. Ages 12–15

Kilodavis, Cheryl. <u>My Princess Boy</u>. Illustrated by Suzanne DeSimone. Simon & Schuster, 2011. 36 pages. Ages 3–7

Mike, Nadia. <u>Leah's Mustache Party</u>. Illustrated by Charlene Chua. Inhabit Media, 2016. 26 pages. Ages 3–7

Silverberg, Cory. <u>Sex Is a Funny Word: A Book About Bodies, Feelings, and YOU</u>. Illustrated by Fiona Smyth. Seven Stories Press, 2015. 159 pages. Ages 8–13

Walliams, David. <u>The Boy in the Dress</u>. Illustrated by Quentin Blake. U.S. edition: Razorbill, 2009. 240 pages. Ages 9–13

Board Books

Biggs, Brian. <u>Tinyville Town: I'm a Librarian</u>. 2017. 22 p. Abrams Appleseed (9781419723223). **Pre+.** A town librarian helps a patron find a book.

Blackstone, Stella and Sunny Scribens. <u>Baby's First Words</u>. Illus. by Christiane Engel. 2017. 30 p. Barefoot Books (9781782853213). **Ages 1–2.** Two dads and their baby spend a busy day together learning new words.

Picture Books

Anderson, Airlie. <u>Neither.</u> 2018. 40 p. Little Brown Books for Young Readers (9780316547697). **Grades Pre-K to 2**
In the Land of This and That, where does Neither belong? Neither finds acceptance in The Land of All.

Bundo, Marlon and Twiss, Jill. <u>A Day in the Life of Marlon Bundo</u>. 2018. 40 p. Chronicle Books (9781452173801). **Grades K and up**
Marlon Bundo is Bunny of the United States, living a comfy life in the White House. In this political satire for all ages, Marlon and newfound love Wesley work together with their animal friends to vote out The Stink Bug.

Cumming, Alan and Grant Shaffer. <u>The Adventures of Honey & Leon</u>. 2017. 48 p. Random House Books for Young Readers (9780399557972). **Grades Pre-K to 3**
Dogs Honey and Leon have a great life in New York—except that they are left behind when their dads travel. They secretly follow them on their next trip.

Finch, Michelle and Phoenix. <u>Phoenix Goes to School</u>. 2018. 40 p. Jessica Kingsley Publishers (9781785928215). **Grades K to 3**
Phoenix is a little worried about her first day of school; what if the other kids call her a boy or don't understand her? Phoenix braves her first day and discovers a warm, accepting environment in the classroom.

Genhart, Michael. <u>Love Is Love.</u> Sourcebooks Jabberwocky/Little Pickle Press (9781939775139). **Grades Pre-K to 3**
A young narrator with two dads is teased for wearing a t-shirt with a rainbow heart. Colorful illustrations highlight a diverse community, affirming the power of love.

Haack, Daniel and Lewis, Stevie. <u>Prince & Knight</u>. 2018. 40 p. little bee books (9781499805529). **Grades Pre-K to 3**
The Prince and the Knight meet when they have to defeat a terrifying dragon, and their friendship blossoms into love.

Jenkins, Steve and Derek Walter. <u>The True Adventures of Esther the Wonder Pig</u>. 2018. 40 p. Little Brown Books for Young Readers (9780316554763). **Grades Pre-K to 3**

Based on a true story, Esther is just a tiny piglet when her dads adopt her, but she turns out to be less of a mini pig and more of a huge pig. As she grows (and grows and grows), Esther shows her family how easy it is to fall in love.

Loney, Andrea J. Bunnybear. Illus. by Carmen Saldaña. 2017. 32 p. Albert Whitman (9780807509388). Pre-Grade 2
Bunnybear is a bear who feels like a bunny but doesn't seem to fit in with either the bunnies or the bears. When he meets Grizzlybun, the two help each other find their place in the world.

Love, Jessica. Julián Is a Mermaid. 2018. 40 p. Candlewick (9780763690458). Grades Pre-K to 3
This lushly-illustrated picture book tells the story of Julián who, with the help of his abuela, dresses up and joins the Coney Island Mermaid Parade.

Martínez, Ernesto J., Maya C. Gonzalez, and Feliciano J. G. Martínez. Cuando Amamos Cantamos/When We Love Someone We Sing to Them. 2018. 39 p. Reflection Press (9781945289149). Grades K and up
Andrea asks his father to help him sing a love song for another boy. His father suggests that they create a new song that they can perform together.

O'Leary, Sara. A Family Is a Family Is a Family. Illus. by Qin Leng. 2016. 32 p. Groundwood (9781554987948). K-Grade 2
When a class discusses their families, one child fears that her family.

Pitman, Gayle E. A Church for All. 2018. 32 p. Albert Whitman & Company (978080751179). Grades Pre-K to 3
Inspired by a real San Francisco church, this story describes a welcoming, inclusive congregation using short rhymes and colorful, diverse illustrations.

Pitman, Gayle E. Sewing the Rainbow. 2018. 32 p. Magination Press (9781433829024). Grades Pre-K to 3
Growing up, Gilbert Baker loved sewing and design. He left Kansas for the bright colors of San Francisco to pursue his dreams and went on to create an enduring symbol of the LGBTQIAP+ community.

Sanders, Rob. Pride: The Story of Harvey Milk and the Rainbow Flag. 2018. 48 p. Random House Books for Young Readers (9780399555312). Grades 1–3
As an elected official, Harvey Milk worked with his community in San Francisco to create a symbol for gay rights and continued fighting for equality until his assassination.

Scotto, Thomas. Jerome by Heart. 2018. 32 p. Enchanted Lion Books (9781592702503) Grades Pre-K to 3
Raphael enjoys his friendship with Jerome: they hold hands, share snacks, and do everything together. Not everyone understands their relationship, but Raphael doesn't mind because he knows how he feels about Jerome.

Middle-Grade Fiction

Bell, Eric. <u>Alan Cole Is Not a Coward.</u> 2017. 272 p. HarperCollins/ Katherine Tegen (9780062567024). Grades 5–7.
In this darkly funny novel about bullying and troubling family dynamics, Alan is blackmailed by his brother while coming to terms with his sexual identity.

Bigelow, Lisa Jenn. <u>Drum Roll, Please.</u> 2018. 320 p. Harper Collins (9780062791146). Grades 5–8
Melly hopes that a week at music camp with her best friend Olivia will distract her from the sudden announcement of her parents' divorce. Although disappointed when they're not placed in the same band, they each discover unexpected feelings for their bandmates.

Bunker, Lisa. <u>Felix Yz.</u> 2017. 288 p. Viking (9780425288504). Grades 5–8
Felix is fused with a fourth dimensional alien and is counting down the days until a potentially fatal experimental surgery to separate them, all the while dealing with his crush on his classmate Hector.

Callender, Kheryn. <u>Hurricane Child.</u> 2018. 224 p. Scholastic Press (9781338129304). Grades 5–8
Caroline is alone: her mother has disappeared and her only friend is a spirit that no one else can see. Then she falls for new student Kalinda, who helps her track down her mother in the middle of a hurricane.

Dee, Barbara. <u>Star-Crossed.</u> 2017. 288 p. Aladdin (9781481478489). Grades 4–8
In her middle school's production of *Romeo & Juliet*, Mattie chooses to play Paris because her crush, Gemma, is cast as Juliet.

Donne, Elena Delle. <u>Elle of the Ball.</u> 2018. 160 p. Simon & Schuster Books for Young Readers (9781534412316). Grades 5–8
Elle loves basketball but she doesn't love the mandatory school dance coming up. She would rather dance with new girl Amanda than with the boys in her class.

Federle, Tim. <u>Nate Expectations.</u> 2018. 256 p. Simon & Schuster Books for Young Readers (9781481404139). Grades 6 and up
When Nate's Broadway show closes, he is forced to go back to his boring hometown for freshman year. But drama follows Nate wherever he goes, in the form of class projects, musical theater, and a cute boy.

Herring Blake, Ashley. <u>Ivy Aberdeen's Letter to the World.</u> 2018. 320 p. Little, Brown Books for Young Readers (9780316515467). Grades 5–8
Ivy Aberdeen's house is destroyed by a tornado, leaving her to navigate a crush on a new friend during the turmoil that her family is thrown into as they try to put their lives back together.

Jantha, A. W. <u>Hocus Pocus and the All New Sequel.</u> Freeform (9781368020039). Grades 7 and up

Poppy and her friends, including her crush Isabella, have just reawakened the Sanderson Sisters. (This book begins with a novelization of the original 1993 film.)

Wittlinger, Ellen. <u>Saturdays with Hitchcock.</u> 2018. 262 p. Charlesbridge (9781580897754). Grades 5–8

Maisie (or "Hitchcock," as she's known to her Uncle Walt) and her best friend Cyrus love seeing old movies on Saturdays. But when new boy Gary starts joining their outings, things change.

Young-Adult Nonfiction

Bongiovanni, Archie and Tristan Jimerson. <u>A Quick & Easy Guide to They/Them Pronouns.</u> 2018. 64 p. Limerence (9781620104996). Grades 6 and up

This comic by real-life friends Archie and Tristan offers readers a practical guide about how, when, and why to use gender-neutral pronouns.

Johnson, Maureen, editor. <u>How I Resist: Activism and Hope for the Next Generation.</u> 2018. 224 p. Wednesday Books (9781250168368). Grades 9 and up

This personal, creative, and deeply hopeful book features words of wisdom and guidance from writers and artists like Alex Gino, Malinda Lo, Jacqueline Woodson, and many more.

MacCarald, Clara. <u>Beating Bullying at Home and in Your Community.</u> 2018. 64 p. Rosen Young Adult (9781508174240). Grades 7 and up

A straightforward guide that describes the types of bullying LGBTQIAP+ kids face as well as realistic responses.

Klein, Rebecca T. <u>Transgender Rights and Protections (Transgender Life).</u> 2017. 64 p. Rosen (9781499464603). Grades 7+

This short book provides succinct information on the transgender rights movement and on legal developments in the areas of employment, health care, education, bathrooms, and more.

Mardell, Ashley. <u>The ABC's of LGBT+.</u> 2016. 190 p. Mango Media (9781633534094). Grades 7+

Mardell's self-published reference book is an introductory text that looks at incredibly complex issues from both theoretical and anecdotal perspectives.

Mooney, Carla. <u>Caitlyn Jenner (Transgender Pioneers).</u> 2017. 112 p. Rosen (9781508171584). Grades 7+

A short biography of Caitlyn Jenner that chronicles her transformation from gold medal athlete to controversial public figure.

Nicholson, Hope, editor. <u>The Secret Loves of Geeks.</u> 2018. 136 p. Dark Horse Comics (9781506704739) Grades 9 and up

A collection of essays, some illustrated and some not, about love–romantic, fandom, or both.

Slater, Dashka. <u>The 57 Bus.</u> 2017. 320 p. Farrar, Straus, and Giroux (9780374303235). Grades 7–12

Sasha is an agender white teen living in a middle-class suburban neighborhood of Oakland, California, Richard is a black teen living in a crime-plagued part of the city. One afternoon, their paths cross on the 57 bus, with disastrous results. Based on a true story, the book is written in a documentary style.

Young-Adult Fiction

Blake, Ashley Herring. <u>Girl Made of Stars.</u> 2018. 304 p. HMH Books for Young Readers (978-1328778239). Grades 9 and up

Mara is dealing with a difficult breakup with her ex-girlfriend when her twin brother is accused of rape by one of her best friends. She struggles with her own past trauma and pressure to maintain the status quo.

Kann, Claire. <u>Let's Talk about Love.</u> 2018. 288 p. Swoon Reads (9781250136121). Grades 9 and up

Alice is asexual and biromantic, which is something she's been dumped for in the past. She was not expecting to fall head over heels for Takumi, a fellow library employee.

Karcz, Lauren. <u>The Gallery of Unfinished Girls.</u> 2017. HarperTeen (9780062467775). Grades 9 and up

Mercedes Moreno hasn't been able to paint in a year, her Abuela is in a coma, and she has an unrequited crush on her best friend, Victoria. Her life takes an unexpected turn when she visits the Red Mangrove Estate: a magical space where art can be created but can never leave.

Khorram, Adib. <u>Darius the Great Is Not Okay.</u> 2018. 310 p. Dial Books (9780525552963). Grades 7 and up

Darius struggles with bullies, depression, and his weight. When he goes to Iran for the first time, Darius makes connections to his Persian heritage and forges a friendship with neighbor Sohrab.

LaCour, Nina. <u>We Are Okay.</u> 2017. 240 p. Dutton (9780525425892). Grades 9–12

After the sudden loss of her grandfather, Marin moves to college, isolating herself from her past. When her best friend Mabel comes to visit during winter break, she is forced to come face-to-face with her grief.

Murphy, Julie. <u>Ramona Blue.</u> 2017. 400 p. HarperCollins/Balzer+Bray (9780062418357). Grades 9–12

Blue-haired teenager Ramona works odd jobs to help support her family in a town that hasn't quite recovered after Hurricane Katrina. Although she identifies as a lesbian, Ramona is thrown for a loop as she realizes her feelings for Freddie, her male best friend.

Ngan, Natasha. <u>Girls of Paper and Fire.</u> 2018. 400 p. JIMMY Patterson Books (9780316561365) Grades 9 and up

In a fantasy world where there are humans, demons, and human-demons, Lei is forcibly taken to become a concubine to the demon king. She must survive violence and rape with her fellow courtesans, who learn to reclaim themselves and fight for their freedom.

Rosen, L. C. <u>Jack of Hearts (and Other Parts).</u> 2018. 342 p. Little, Brown (9780316480536). Grades 10 and up

Jack is an unabashedly out, sex-positive high school junior living large in New York. When he reluctantly agrees to write a sex advice column for a friend's blog, he also starts receiving "love letters" that become increasingly threatening in tone.

Silvera, Adam. <u>They Both Die at the End.</u> 2017. 384 p. HarperTeen (9780062457790). Grades 9–12

Mateo and Rufus both find out that they are going to die today. Over the course of the day, their stories and lives converge. Starting as a search for a final friendship, the boys develop a relationship far deeper than either of them expected.

Stevens, Courtney. <u>Dress Codes for Small Towns.</u> 2017. 352 p. HarperTeen (9780062398512). Grades 9–12

Billie McCaffrey—artist, preacher's daughter, and general troublemaker—finds herself in an awkward position when she and her four best friends accidentally burn down a section of their church. The friends, and Billie in particular, find themselves in the spotlight as they work to save the cherished harvest festival and stay out of trouble.

Stone, Nic. <u>Odd One Out.</u> 2018. 320 p. Crown Books for Young Readers (9781101939536). Grades 9–12

Coop has feelings for his lifelong bestie Jupiter but knows nothing will ever happen between them because she is a lesbian. When Rae moves to town and joins their tight twosome, all their feelings collide in this messy, realistic story about falling in love, new romance, and friendship.

Albertalli, Becky. <u>Leah on the Offbeat.</u> 2018. 368 p. HarperCollins/Balzer + Bray (9780062643803). Grades 9 and up

Leah Burke must navigate first love, her college search, and the unexpected implosion of her once-unshakable friend group. She's also bisexual but she can't find the right way to come out to her friends.

Albertalli, Becky and Adam Silvera. <u>What If It's Us.</u> 2018. 448 p. HarperTeen (9780062795250). Grades 9 and up

Arthur wants to find a relationship and Ben wants to get over his ex. After a serendipitous meeting they discover the reality of romance together.

Albertalli, Becky. <u>The Upside of Unrequited.</u> 2017. 352 p. HarperCollins/ Balzer+Bray (9780062348708). Grades 9–12

With same-sex marriage now legalized in the United States, twins Cassie and Molly's moms are tying the knot. But, as Cassie and Molly each enter into new romantic relationships, the sisters begin to grow apart.

Armentrout, Jennifer L., et al. <u>Meet Cute.</u> 2018. 320 p. HMH Books for Young Readers (978-1328604286). Grades 7 and up

A fun short story collection featuring a variety of romantic relationships.

Benway, Robin. <u>Far from the Tree.</u> 2017. 384 p. HarperTeen (9780062330682). Grades 8–11

Three siblings, two adopted and one in the foster system, form tenuous bond while trying to cope with life's many obstacles.

Berube, Amelinda. <u>The Dark Beneath the Ice.</u> 2018. 336 p. Sourcebooks Fire (9781492657071). Grades 9 and up

Marianne begins to experience scary paranormal phenomena as her parents are undergoing a divorce. After an attempted exorcism with her new friend Rhiannon, Marianne is not sure that she and the people she loves will survive this haunting.

Booth, Molly. <u>Nothing Happened.</u> 2018. 336 p. Disney Hyperion (9781484753026). Grades 9 and up

In this retelling of Shakespeare's comedy *Much Ado About Nothing*, camp counselors Bee and Ben Snark and flirt while shy Hana and Claudia battle their own insecurities to try to get together.

Brennan, Sarah Rees. <u>In Other Lands.</u> 2017. 432 p. Big Mouth House (978-1618731203). Grades 9 and up

Elliot is recruited to a magical school in a magical land and works to upend the system's violent ways while navigating relationships with the classmates and creatures of this new place.

Callender, Kheryn. <u>This Is Kind of an Epic Love Story.</u> 2018. 304 p. Balzer + Bray (9780062820228). Grades 10 and up

Nathan and his ex-girlfriend have remained good friends even after their breakup. Their social group is complicated when Nate's childhood friend (and secret crush) moves back to town.

Cameron, Sophie. <u>Out of the Blue.</u> 2018. 272 p. Roaring Brook Press (9781250149916). Grades 7 and up

Mysterious beings are falling from the sky to their deaths. When Jaya finds one alive, she enlists new friends to help her keep the being safe.

Capetta, Amy Rose. <u>Echo after Echo.</u> 2017. 432 p. Candlewick (9780763691646). Grades 9 and up

Zara moves to New York City, where she has the opportunity to play the role she's always coveted. Unfortunately, not everyone is as excited about the production, as cast members begin to die under mysterious circumstances.

Carter, Brooke. <u>Learning Seventeen.</u> 2018. 134 p. Orca (9781459815537). Grades 8 and up

Jane rebels against the rules of religious reform school, where she is encouraged to suppress her sexuality. Ultimately, she finds love, acceptance, and family reconciliation.

Cherry, Alison, Lindsay Ribar, and Michelle Schusterman. <u>The Pros of Cons.</u> 2018. 341 p. Point/Scholastic (9781338151725). Grades 7 and up

Worlds collide when Phoebe's school band competition, Vanessa's fandom con, and the taxidermy convention Callie is attending with her father are all at the same hotel and convention center.

Cohn, Rachel, and David Levithan. <u>Sam and Ilsa's Last Hurrah.</u> 2018. 224 p. Knopf Books for Young Readers (9780399553844). Grades 7 and up

Twins Sam and Ilsa throw an intimate dinner party and each invites three guests—but the other does not know who has been invited.

Colbert, Brandy. <u>Little & Lion.</u> 2017. 336 p. Little, Brown (9780316349000). Grades 9–12

Suzette and her stepbrother navigate their tenuous relationship while also dealing with the fact that they have feelings for the same girl. To make things more complicated, her stepbrother has been diagnosed with bipolar disorder.

Cotugno, <u>Katie. Top Ten.</u> 2017. 368 p. Balzer + Bray (9780062418302). Grades 9 and up

On graduation night, best friends Ryan and Gabby look back on the top ten memories of their high school friendships, fights, and romantic attractions.

Coulthurst, Audrey. <u>Inkmistress.</u> 2018. 400 p. Balzer + Bray (978-0062433282). Grades 9 and up

Asra's power to change fate by writing in her blood sets off a chain of events that puts her in direct opposition to her love, Ina.

Daniels, April. <u>Nemesis, Book 1: Dreadnought.</u> 2017. 276 p. Diversion (9781682300688). Grades 7+

Danny Tozer is a closeted trans girl until she gets the powers of Dreadnought, a legacy superhero. With the powers comes a transformation that can't hide who she really is, much to the dismay of her family.

Daniels, April. <u>Nemesis, Book 2: Sovereign.</u> 2017. 314 p. Diversion (9781682308240). Grades 7+

In Danny's second adventure, she comes head to head with a white supremacist and a Trans-Exclusionary Radical Feminist (TERF).

Dietrich, Cale. <u>The Love Interest.</u> 2017. 384 p. Feiwel and Friends (9781250107138). Grades 9–12

In an alternate universe where perfect mates are cultivated for their partners, two potential love interests, Dylan and Caden, end up interested in each other.

Dooley, Sarah. <u>Ashes to Asheville.</u> 2017. 256 p. Putnam (9780399165047). Grades 4–7

Two sisters, separated after the death of one of their mothers, end up together on a road trip to spread her ashes.

Farizan, Sara. <u>Here to Stay.</u> 2018. 272 p. Algonquin Young Readers (9781616207007). Grades 9 and up

After Iranian-Jordanian Bijan makes a game-winning basket, his new-found fame leads to unwanted attention. When an anonymous picture of him photoshopped to look like a terrorist goes viral, Bijan must figure out how to stand up for what is right—for himself and his friends.

Fine, Sarah. <u>The Cursed Queen.</u> 2017. 432 p. Simon & Schuster/Margaret K. McElderry (9781481441933). Grades 8–12

Ansa has fought for her place in her tribe, and now she must fight against her own body as magic threatens to take her over.

Floreen, Tim. <u>Tattoo Atlas.</u> 2016. 384 p. Simon & Schuster (9781481432801). Grades 9–12

In this sci-fi thriller, Rem's scientist mother attempts to cure a sociopathic classmate responsible for the murder of Rem's best friend. But can evil be cured?

Foody, Amanda. <u>Ace of Shades.</u> 2018. 416 p. Harlequin Teen (978-1335692290). Grades 9 and up

Enne searches for her mother in New Reynes, the "City of Sin," using only a name her mother mentioned in her last letter: Levi, a young, charismatic street lord and con artist.

Forman, Gayle. <u>I Have Lost My Way.</u> 2018. 272 p. Viking Books for Young Readers (9780425290774). Grades 9 and up

Freya, Harun, and Nathaniel have all suffered significant loss. Their lives intersect in New York City one fateful day, and they work together to heal.

Friend, Natasha. <u>The Other F-Word.</u> 2017. 336 p. Farrar, Straus, and Giroux (9780374302344). Grades 9–12

Hollis and Milo have two things in common: they were both conceived with sperm from the same donor, and they both have two moms. Together they begin a journey that leads them to other half-siblings and walks them through grief, friendship, and the meaning of family.

Gardner, Whitney. <u>Chaotic Good.</u> 2018. 256 p. Knopf Books for Young Readers (9781524720803). Grades 7 and up

Cameron uses her cosplay talents and her twin brother's wardrobe to pass as a boy so she isn't mocked by the employees at her local comic book shop. When her new alter ego is invited to join their D&D group, she is asked out by Why, who is gay.

Gilbert, Kelly Loy. <u>Picture Us in the Light.</u> 2018. 368 p. Disney Hyperion (9781484726020). Grades 9 and up

Danny expresses himself through his art. But his art won't make it clear to him why his friend completed suicide, what his parents are hiding, and what's going on with his best friend Harry.

Gonsalves, Florence. <u>Love and Other Carnivorous Plants.</u> 2018. 352 p. Little Brown (978-0316436724). Grades 9 and up

Danny and her best friend Sara have their lives all planned out. But those plans are derailed when Danny gets into Harvard for pre-med and secretly enters rehab for an eating disorder, where she discovers an attraction to a fellow patient.

Howard, Greg. <u>Social Intercourse.</u> 2018. 309 p. Simon & Schuster (9781481497817). Grades 10 and up

Beckett, an out and proud high schooler desperate to lose his virginity, and Jaxon, a popular jock with a cute girlfriend, discover their parents are dating and complicate things by falling for each other.

Hutchinson, Shaun David. <u>At the Edge of the Universe.</u> 2017. 496 p. Simon Pulse (9781481449663). Grades 9–12

Ozzie thinks the universe is slowly shrinking after his boyfriend, Tommy, disappears. Together with his self-destructive classmate Calvin, they investigate the disappearance. Is the universe really shrinking? Or has Ozzie lost his mind?

Hutchinson, Shaun David. <u>The Apocalypse of Elena Mendoza.</u> 2018. 448 p. Simon Pulse (9781481498548). Grades 9 and up

Elena's mother was a virgin when she was conceived. Now, as a teenager, Elena has healing powers, but every time she uses them other people disappear, and inanimate objects speak to her.

Ius, Dawn. <u>Lizzie.</u> 2018. 336 p. Simon Pulse (9781481490764). Grades 7 and up

In this imaginative modern retelling of Lizzie Borden's story, Lizzie is shy, never been kissed, and controlled by her parents. When she meets Bridget, the family's new maid, she quickly falls in love.

Jones, Adam Garnet. <u>Fire Song</u>. 2018. 232 p. Annick Press (9781554519781). Grades 9 and up

Shane's life on the Anishinaabe reserve isn't easy. After the recent suicide of his sister, he finds solace in his secret relationship with David.

Kisner, Adrienne. <u>Dear Rachel Maddow</u>. 2018. 263 p. Feiwel and Friends (9781250146021). Grades 7 and up

School doesn't come naturally to Brynn Harper. After her brother's drug-related death, she stops trying. Stuck in remedial courses and considering dropping out to escape an abusive household, Brynn discovers a spark of passion in an unlikely place: school politics.

Konigsberg, Bill. <u>Honestly Ben</u>. 2017. 336 p. Scholastic/Arthur A. Levine (9780545858267). Grades 9–12

School is tough, and star athlete Ben can't quite figure out what's going on with his sexuality. Is he gay, bi, or "straight with a twist"?

Lauren, Christina. <u>Autoboyography</u>. 2017. 416 p. Simon & Schuster (9781481481687). Grades 9–12

Senior Tanner Scott enrolls in Provo High's infamous Seminar, which tasks students with writing a book in a semester's time. Little does Tanner know that this class will introduce him to Sebastian Brother, a practicing Mormon whose smile ruins him at first sight.

Lawson, Richard. <u>All We Can Do Is Wait</u>. 2018. 288 p. Razorbill (9780448494111). Grades 7 and up

After a bridge collapses, teens bond in a hospital waiting area while dreading the fates of their loved ones.

Lee, C. B. <u>Not Your Villain</u>. 2017. 320 p. Interlude Press (9781945053252). Grades 7 and up

Bells is leveling up to superhero—if the bigger heroes don't stand in his way, in this sequel to *Not Your Sidekick*.

Lee, Mackenzi. <u>The Gentleman's Guide to Vice and Virtue</u>. 2017. 528 p. HarperCollins/Katherine Tegen (9780062382801). Grades 9–12

Henry Montague sets off on his European grand tour with best friend and crush, Percy. The young men embark on a whirlwind journey filled with crime, angst, adventure, and learned secrets.

Lee, Mackenzi. <u>The Lady's Guide to Petticoats and Piracy</u>. 2018. 450 p. Katherine Tegen Books (9780062795328). Grades 7 and up

Felicity Montague wants to become a doctor, but the men of 18th-century Edinburgh and London won't have her. She decides to appeal to her medical hero, but to do so she must reconcile with her childhood best friend, leading to adventures and intrigue across Europe.

Leno, Katrina. <u>Summer of Salt.</u> 2018. 256 p. HarperTeen (9780062493620). Grades 6 and up

The women in Georgina's family have all inherited a special ability and she worries she has been passed over by the magic as she approaches her 18th birthday. Before she leaves her island home for college, a mystical tragedy about the death of a rare bird rips apart the town and her relationship with her twin sister. CW: rape.

Lo, Malinda. <u>A Line in the Dark.</u> 2017. 288 p. Speak (9780735227439). Grades 9 and up

Jess has unrequited feelings for her best friend Angie and struggles with jealousy when Angie starts up a relationship with rich girl Margot. Secrets and violence are hiding under the surface of all their lives.

Lukens, F. T. <u>The Rules and Regulations for Mediating Myths and Magic.</u> 2018. 304 p. Interlude Press (9781945053245). Grades 9 and up

Bridger needs to pay for college, but the unusual job he finds on Craigslist has him dealing with cranky unicorns, mermaids, and other mysterious creatures. On top of everything else, he must navigate the tricky process of coming out.

Lundin, Britta. <u>Ship It.</u> 2018. 384 p. Freeform (9781368003131). Grades 9 and up

Claire writes slash fiction based on her favorite TV show, *Demon Heart*, and she's convinced that her ship should go canon. But when she confronts the show's actors and producers at a convention, Claire risks losing everything she cares about, including her new romance with fellow fan, Tess.

Mac, Carrie. <u>10 Things I Can See from Here.</u> 2017. 320 p. Knopf (9780399556258). Grades 9–12

Maeve is really anxious … all the time! She obsessively imagines the most drastic of scenarios. Just when she thinks things can't get any worse, her mother has to go away for six months, leaving Maeve to go reluctantly live with her alcoholic dad.

Marsh, Sarah Glenn. <u>Reign of the Fallen.</u> 2018. 384 p. Razorbill (9780448494395). Grades 7 and up

Karthia is ruled by untouchable dead royals, and Odessa, a necromancer, must traverse the land of the dead and uncover the truth when a series of attacks reveal that whole kingdom is in jeopardy.

McGuire, Seanan. <u>Down among the Sticks and Bones.</u> 2017. 192 p. Tor (9780765392039). Grades 7–12

This prequel to *Every Heart a Doorway* follows Jack and Jill into their magical world and chronicles the resulting experiences as one sister is apprenticed to a mad scientist, and the other lives a life of quiet, tragic beauty.

McLemore, Anna-Marie. <u>Wild Beauty.</u> 2017. 352 p. Feiwel & Friends (9781250124555). Grades 7 and up
The Nomeolvides women have lived in La Pradera for generations growing lush magical gardens, but their family is cursed—destined to lose anyone they love too deeply. When Estrella and her cousins realize they are all in love with the same girl, they make offerings to the land in an attempt to save her. The land responds with the appearance of a boy with no memories, whose past holds the key to generations of secrets and lies.

McNamara, Miriam. <u>The Unbinding of Mary Reade.</u> 2018. 280 p. Sky Pony Press (9781510727052). Grades 9 and up
Mary Reade dresses as a man to sneak into a life of piracy but is stunned when she meets Anne Bonny, a pirate who is not afraid to hide her gender. Mary deals with her gender dysphoria, strong feelings for Anne, and sexual identity as she tries to survive.

Mele, Dana. <u>People Like Us.</u> 2018. 384 p. Putnam (9781524741709). Grades 9 and up
Running from a secret past, Kay has remade her life at posh Bates Academy. But when a student's body is found in a nearby lake, Kay's tragic past and ruthless methods make her a prime suspect in a murder—and the target of blackmail threatening to expose her past.

Miller, Linsey. <u>Mask of Shadows.</u> 2017. 352 p. Sourcebooks Fire (9781492647492). Grades 9 and up
Seeking revenge on the nobles responsible for the destruction of their people, genderfluid pickpocket Sal decides to audition for a position on the Queen's Left Hand, Her Majesty's royal assassins. The competition is fierce, and the body count is high.

Miller, Sam J. <u>The Art of Starving.</u> 2017. 384 p. HarperTeen (9780062456717). Grades 9–12
Matt has an eating disorder. He is also dealing with bullying and developing a crush on classmate Tariq. To make things even more bizarre, he is pretty sure that eating less is giving him supernatural powers.

Mitchell, Saundra. <u>All Out: The No-Longer-Secret Stories of Queer Teens throughout the Ages.</u> 2018. 241 p. Harlequin Teen (9781335470454). Grades 7 and up
Seventeen short historical fiction stories about queer experiences across many time periods and cultures.

Ness, Patrick. <u>Release.</u> 2017. 288 p. Harper Teen (9780062403193). Grades 9 and up
Adam Thorn is having the most unsettling, difficult day of his life, with relationships fracturing, a harrowing incident at work, and a showdown with his

preacher father that changes everything. It's a day of confrontation, running, sex, love, heartbreak, disturbing visions, and maybe even hope.

Nijkamp, Marieke. <u>Before I Let Go.</u> 2018. 368 p. Sourcebooks Fire (9781492642282). Grades 9 and up

Back in her small, strange hometown in Alaska, Corey is determined to find out what really happened to her best friend. But the whole town is pushing her away, which only makes her more determined to seek the truth.

Ormsbee, Kathryn. <u>Tash Hearts Tolstoy.</u> 2017. 384 p. Simon & Schuster (9781481489331). Grades 9–12

When Tash's webcast based on *Anna Karenina* goes viral, she must balance fame, a frantic filming schedule, sibling rivalry, and deciding whether to come out as a romantic asexual to the boy she likes.

Oseman, Alice. <u>Radio Silence.</u> 2017. 496 p. HarperTeen (9780062335715). Grades 8–12

At school, Frances is studious and aiming for Cambridge, but at home, she's a quirky artist hooked on her favorite podcast, Universe City. When she is invited to collaborate with its quiet creator, she begins to truly discover herself.

Oshiro, Mark. <u>Anger Is a Gift.</u> 2018. 464 p. Tor Teen (9781250167026). Grades 9 and up

When Moss was a child, his father was shot by the Oakland police. Now, as racial tensions are building in his high school, Moss falls for Javier. When Moss decides he wants to take a stand, he risks losing everything.

Patterson, Kaitlyn Sage. <u>The Diminished.</u> 2018. 454 p. Harlequin Teen (9781335016416). Grades 7 and up

In a world where babies are born in pairs, Bo is a single born, destined for the throne while Vi is "diminished," her twin having died when they were very young. As their lives intersect, they will discover secrets that will change them both.

Philips, L. <u>Perfect Ten.</u> 2017. 352 p. Viking (9780425288115). Grades 8–11

Two years after Sam broke up with his boyfriend, his dating prospects seem grim. When his best friend Meg, a Wiccan, suggests a love spell, Sam is willing to try anything. But he gets more than he bargained for.

Podos, Rebecca. <u>Like Water.</u> 2017. 320 p. HarperCollins/Balzer+Bray (9780062373373). Grades 9–12

Vanni's father has Huntington's disease, so there's a chance she will too. In order to be there for her family, she puts off her future to stay in the New Mexico town she's always wanted to leave. But when Vanni meets Leigh, she realizes there are new things to learn even in their sleepy town.

Poston, Ashley. Heart of Iron. 2018. 480 p. Balzer + Bray (9780062652850). Grades 9 and up

Ana and her found family of thieves make a living doing whatever jobs they can get when Ana's best friend D09 needs her help. In a desperate bid to save him, she meets a rich, spoiled Ironblood, and together they track down a ship that may have all the answers they need.

Redgate, Riley. Final Draft. 2018. 262 p. Amulet (9781419728723). Grades 9 and up

Laila loves writing sci-fi stories, but a demanding new creative writing teacher pushes her to work harder and do more. Caught between confusing crushes, a headstrong best friend, and demands of school and family, Laila struggles to figure it all out.

Roehrig, Caleb. Last Seen Leaving. 2016. 336 p. Feiwel and Friends (9781250085634). Grades 9–12

Flynn's girlfriend, January, has been missing and he is the chief suspect. When January's bloody clothes are found, indicating the possibility of her murder, forensic tests show that she was pregnant. What everyone doesn't know is that Flynn never consummated his relationship with January because he has been hiding a secret: his sexuality.

Roehrig, Caleb. White Rabbit. 2018. 336 p. Feiwel and Friends (9781250085658). Grades 7 and up

To save his sister, Rufus has to solve a murder, fast. Unfortunately, his ex-boyfriend decides to come along for the ride, and that's only the first surprise.

Rubin, Julia Lynn. Burro Hills. 2018. 244 p. Diversion Books (9781635761948). Grades 9 and up

Jack can no longer hide his sexuality when Connor comes to town. But is Connor a bad boy leading him astray or the guy of his dreams?

Self, Jeffrey. A Very, Very Bad Thing. 2017. 240 p. Scholastic/Push (9781338118407) Grades 8–12

Marley has to decide whether it's best to own up to a lie he told or continue to perpetuate it for what might be a greater good.

Shaw, Liane. Caterpillars Can't Swim. 2018. 246 p. Second Story Press (9781772600537). Grades 9 and up

Ryan, a high school swimmer who uses a wheelchair, rescues Jack from drowning and the two become unlikely friends. Their friendship allows Jack to finally admit he's gay and make strides toward self-acceptance despite the judgments of his community.

Silvera, Adam. History Is All You Left Me. 2017. 304 p. Soho Teen (9781616956929). Grades 9–12

OCD-afflicted Griffin has just lost his first love, Theo. In an attempt to hold onto every piece of the past, he forges a friendship with Theo's last boyfriend,

Jackson. When Jackson begins to exhibit signs of guilt, Griffin suspects he's hiding something and will stop at nothing to get to the truth.

Sim, Tara. <u>Chainbreaker.</u> 2018. 488 p. Sky Pony Press (9781510706194). Grades 9 and up

In a reimagined world where time's passing is dependent on the spirits that inhabit clock towers, mechanic Danny is sent to India to investigate a city whose tower was destroyed but time never stopped.

Spalding, Amy. <u>The Summer of Jordi Perez (and the Best Burger in Los Angeles).</u> 2018. 284 p. Sky Pony Press (9780316515467). Grades 8 and up

Body-positive Abby lands the internship of her dreams with a fashion boutique only to find out she has to share it with classmate Jordi Perez. She has to deal with her growing feelings for Jordi while also competing with her for a coveted paid position.

Spotswood, Jessica. <u>The Last Summer of the Garrett Girls.</u> 2018. 368 p. Sourcebooks Fire (9781492622192) Grades 6 and up

The Garrett girls have one last summer together in their small town. Oldest sister Des feels left behind, Bea may be changing her mind about her long-time boyfriend, Kat wants her ex back, and Vi has a thing for the girl next door.

Sugiura, Misa. <u>It's Not Like It's a Secret.</u> 2017. 400 p. HarperTeen (9780062473417). Grades 9–12

Sana moves from an all-white Midwest town to California, where she's expected to only be friends with other Asian girls. As she navigates this new culture, she finds herself falling for a Latina girl, and comes to suspect that her father is having an affair.

Surmelis, Angelo. <u>The Dangerous Art of Blending in.</u> 2018. 315 p. HarperCollins/Balzer + Bray (9780062659002). Grades 9 and up

Evan returns from summer camp to discover his best friend Henry has become impossibly attractive. As his feelings for Henry grow more intense, Evan's mother becomes more abusive, and he must find the courage to speak up.

Talley, Robin. <u>Pulp.</u> 2018. 416 p. Harlequin Teen (9781335012906). Grades 9 and up

In the present day, Abby is a high school senior dealing with lingering romantic feelings for her best friend/ex-girlfriend. In 1955, Janet must hide her relationship with her best friend Marie even though she knows there is nothing wrong with their love. Both Abby and Janet find solace in the lesbian pulp novels they read.

Talley, Robin. <u>As I Descended.</u> 2016. 384 p. HarperTeen (9780062409232). Grades 9–12

In this queer revisioning of Macbeth, Maria and Lily are a power couple at their private school. Ghostly accidents start happening after they commune with spirits and madness soon takes over.

Talley, Robin. <u>Our Own Private Universe.</u> 2017. 384 p. HarlequinTeen (9780373211982). Grades 9–12

Aki is in Mexico on a mission trip with her father's church, and her best friend goads her into flirting with a young woman from another church. Aki thinks it's a fling, but what if it turns out to be more?

Trifonia, Melibia Obono. Translated by Lawrence Schimel. <u>La Bastarda.</u> 2018. 120 p. The Feminist Press at CUNY (9781936932238). Grades 7–12

Okomo has always been an outsider due to her mother's death and her father's rejection. When she starts spending time with village outcasts, she can no longer hide or deny who she is.

Watts, Julia. <u>Quiver.</u> 2018. 300 p. Three Rooms Press (9781941110669). Grades 7–9

Libby and Zo come from two very different worlds. Zo is a queer, genderfluid teen from Knoxville and Libby is the eldest of six siblings, living off the grid with her devout Quiverfull family. When Zo's family move next door to Libby, the two slowly become friends, neither expecting how much the friendship will change their lives.

Wilde, Jen. <u>Queens of Geek.</u> 2017. 288 p. Swoon Reads (9781250111395). Grades 7+ Dual narrators Charlie (who is bi and famous) and Taylor (who is anxious and on the autism spectrum) travel from Australia to Los Angeles to attend SupaCon.

Wilde, Jen. <u>The Brightsiders.</u> 2018. 304 p. Swoon Reads (9781250189714). Grades 9 and up

Emmy King is a teenage rock star and lives like one, until a night out with her bandmates and her girlfriend ends with a car crash documented by the paparazzi. As she recovers from her public humiliation, she comes out as bisexual in front of her fans at a concert and she starts to have feelings for her genderfluid bandmate, Alfie.

Woodfolk, Ashley. <u>The Beauty That Remains.</u> 2018. 336 p. Delacorte Press (9781524715878). Grades 9 and up

Unexpected catastrophic loss brings together Autumn, Shay, and Logan: Autumn has lost her best friend, Shay has lost her twin sister, and Logan has lost his ex-boyfriend. Told in alternating perspectives, these three unite through a shared love of music.

Graphic Novels

Steele, Hamish. <u>DeadEndia: The Watcher's Test.</u> 2018. 240 p. Nobrow (9781910620472). Grade 7 and up

Barney's folks kicked him out of the house when he came out as transgender. He lands a custodial job at Pollywood, a haunted amusement park named after a famous movie star, where he and his friends deal with demon possession, zombie cowboys, time travelers, and first love.

Black, Holly, et al. Lumberjanes: Bonus Tracks. 2018. 128 p. BOOM! Box (9781684152162). Grades 5 and up
In this collection of one-shots and specials, the camp friends Lumberjanes embark on stand-alone adventures with magical creatures.

Chii. The Bride Was a Boy. 2018. 158 p. Seven Seas (9781626928886). Grades 7 and up
This memoir shares Chii's process of transition while focusing on her relationship and wedding in Japan.

DiMartino, Michael Dante and Irene Koh. Legend of Korra: Turf Wars Part One. 2017. 80 p. Dark Horse Books (978150670015). Grades 4–8
This comic based on the popular television show kicks off with Korra and Asami building their life together in a very changed world.

Ellis, Grace and Shae Beagle. Moonstruck, Vol. 1: Magic to Brew. 2018. 120 p. Image Comics (9781534304772). Grades 7 and up
Werewolf barista Julie must team up with her new girlfriend Selena (also a werewolf) and clairvoyant friend Cass to save their bubbly centaur friend, Chet, from the effects of a terrible spell.

Franklin, Tee and Jenn St-Onge. Bingo Love. 2018. 88 p. Image Comics (9781534307506). Grades 9 and up
In the 1960s, South, teenagers Hazel and Mari meet and fall in love, but they are ultimately forced to part ways. Decades later, they meet again as grandmothers and rekindle their romance.

Grace, Sina and Vitti Alessandro. Iceman, Vol. 1: Thawing Out. 2018. 136 p. Marvel (9781302908799). Grades 9 and up
Long-time X-Men member Bobby Drake, also known as Iceman, has always been quick to crack a joke–until a teen version of himself is brought to the future and comes out as gay. Now he has to deal with his sexuality, his family, and his exes.

Grace, Sina and Vitti Alessandro. Iceman, Vol. 2: Absolute Zero. 2018. 112 p. Marvel (9781302908805) Grades 9 and up
Bobby Drake, aka Iceman, must contend with Wolverine's son, a new love interest, his old team, and his parents discovering his time-displaced self.

Graley, Sarah. Kim Reaper, Vol. 1: Grim Beginnings. 112 p. Oni Press, 2018. (9781620104552). Grades 9 and up
When Becka finally works up the courage to ask out her university classmate, Kim, she has no idea that Kim has a part-time job helping the Grim Reaper.

Kaye, Julia. Super Late Bloomer: My Early Days in Transition. 2018. 160 p. Andrews McMeel Publishing (9781449489625). Grades 9 and up

Artist Julia Kaye chronicles her transition with charming, light-hearted, three-panel comic strips, originally published as a web series.

Larson, Hope, Jackie Ball, and Noah Hayes. Goldie Vance, Vol. 3. 2017. 112 p. BOOM! Box (9781684150533). Grades 6 and up
Goldie's detective skills are put to the test when she is forced to team up with her rival Sugar Maple to figure out who is sabotaging cars in the big race.

Larson, Hope, Jackie Ball, and Elle Power. Goldie Vance, Vol. 4. 2018. 112 p. BOOM! Box (9781684151400). Grades 7 and up
Mysteries abound leading up to the St. Pascal Rockin' the Beach Music Festival, but Goldie Vance is on the case.

O'Neill, Katie. The Tea Dragon Society. 2017. 72 p. Oni Press (9781620104415). Grades 3–7
An oversized graphic novel that follows blacksmith-in-training Greta as she joins a group that harvests tea and bonds with dragons.

Rivera, Gabby and Joe Quinones. America, Vol. 2: Fast and Fuertona. 2018. 136 p. Marvel (9781302908829). Grades 7 and up
America explores her family history and faces off against a new villain in her continuing adventures.

Rivera, Gabby and Joe Quinones. America, Vol. 1: The Life and Times of America Chavez. 2017. 136 p. Marvel (9781302908812). Grades 7 and up
America Chavez, Young Avenger and leader of the Ultimates, heads off to Sotomayor University, but in the midst of intimidatingly huge class projects, there are Nazis to punch, entitled cyborgs to deprogram, and creepy fan cults to disband.

Rowell, Rainbow and Kris Anka. Runaways, Vol. 1: Find Your Way Home. 2018. 136 p. Marvel (9781302908522). Grades 7 and up
The author of *Fangirl* puts her spin on the new classic Marvel team of teens who discovered their parents were supervillains. Now a few years older, the team has split apart. But when one of their members is back from the dead, maybe it's time for everyone to come back together.

Rowell, Rainbow and Kris Anka. Runaways, Vol. 2: Best Friends Forever. 2018. 136 p. Marvel (9781302911973). Grades 7 and up
Karolina's girlfriend comes to visit, and everyone must adjust to life as a team again.

Sell, Chad, et al. Cardboard Kingdom. 2018. 288 p. Knopf Books for Young Readers (9781524719388). Grades 4 and up
Neighborhood kids use their imaginations and a bounty of cardboard to have the most exciting, heroic summer ever.

Tagame, Gengoroh. <u>My Brother's Husband, Vol. 2.</u> 2018. 351 p. Pantheon (9781101871539). Grades 7 and up

Yaichi, a divorced Japanese father, must face the inherent prejudices of modern Japanese culture and his own feelings when Mike, the Canadian husband of Yaichi's dead brother, comes to stay with Yaichi and his daughter for an extended visit.

Tynion IV, James and Rian Sygh. <u>The Backstagers, Vol. 1.</u> 2017. 112 p. BOOM! Box (9781608869930). Grades 7–12

When Jory transfers to an all-boys private school and joins the Drama club in an attempt to make new friends, he discovers the mysterious world of the backstage.

Usdin, Carly and Vakueva, Nina. <u>Heavy Vinyl.</u> 2018. 112 p. BOOM! Box (9781684151417). Grades 7 and up

The new girl at Heavy Vinyl Records, Chris, doesn't know that the manager and other employees double as a crime-battling, patriarchy-busting female fight club. When the lead singer of Chris's favorite band goes missing, the group brings her in to help solve the mystery—and maybe even get the girl. Numbers 1, 2, 3, and 4 of the new comic book series.

Wang, Jen. <u>The Prince and the Dressmaker.</u> 2018. 288 p. First Second (9781626723634). Grades 7 and up

Prince Sebastian hires talented dressmaker Frances to make gowns for the fabulously fashionable Lady Crystallia, his nighttime alter ego. While Frances loves designing dresses for Sebastian, she isn't sure how long she can keep his secret.

Young, Keezy. <u>Taproot.</u> 2017. 128 p. Lion Forge/Roar (9781941302460). Grades 9–12

Love story meets ghost story in this graphic novel about Blue, a ghost, and Hamal, one of the few humans who can see him.

Index

Printed in the United States
by Baker & Taylor Publisher Services